GUIDED BY THE *Shepherd*

Our Family's Journey through Cancer

VICKIE JETT

Guided by the Shepherd: Our Family's Journey through Cancer

All scripture quotations are taken from the Authorized King James Version (KJV) of the Bible. (Public Domain.)

To place an order, or view other Bible studies, contact may be made at *jettfamilyministry.com* or jettfamilyministry@gmail.com. To read Rachelle's story, visit her website at *GodSaidCancer.com*.

ISBN: 978-0-578-44785-8

Printed in the United States of America

ABOUT THE AUTHOR

Raised in a Christian home in Texas, Vickie was five years of age when she accepted Christ as her personal Savior. She surrendered to full-time service as a teenager. While attending Bible college, she married her husband, Jamie, who was also a student preparing for the ministry. She and her husband enjoy having three children and seven grandchildren and currently reside in Oklahoma.

Vickie and Jamie's ministry together has included almost twenty years in the pastorate in Texas and Wyoming. They have both also served since 1998 at Heartland Baptist Bible College in Oklahoma City as full-time faculty. Vickie teaches various Ladies Classes and Ladies Counseling Classes, as well as speaks at ladies conferences.

Her education experience includes: Western Wyoming College (A.A.), Pacific Coast Baptist Bible College (B.A.), Salt Lake Baptist College (M.A., D.C.M.), Bethhaven Christian Counselor's Seminary (MA., Ph.D.) in Biblical Counseling.

In an effort to assist people who are experiencing problems of living, the Jetts have co-authored a series of biblical counseling guides, which are short Bible studies that assist in finding answers from God's Word. The Jett Counseling Guides are currently available through the Baptist Times. Their hearts' desire is to serve the Lord in helping to encourage, train and provide tools for others in the ministry.

2 Peter 1:3, *"According as his divine power hath given unto us all things that pertain unto life and godliness, through the knowledge of him that hath called us to glory and virtue."*

DEDICATED TO

My wonderful husband
who has travelled this life journey by my side.
He has given unfailing encouragements
for me to write about our family's journey,
and has shown loving patience
each step of the way.

My amazing children
who never gave up and never let go of
the Shepherd's hand!

My Heavenly Father, my eternal Shepherd,
who despite my many failings, never left my side.
I can rejoice in the Lord for making this journey possible,
for entrusting, empowering and enabling us through this
that He may get the glory!

I Timothy 1:12,
*"And I thank Christ Jesus our Lord, who hath enabled me,
for that he counted me faithful, putting me into the ministry."*

ACKNOWLEDGEMENTS

Thank you to our Christian brothers and sisters
who faithfully prayed for our family through the journey.

Thank you to the medical personnel
who, in their various roles, gave of themselves
through the health battles.

Thank you to our many Christian brothers and sisters
who assisted in encouraging, editing and finishing the book.

Thank you to Kaitlyn Tomey
for her setup and cover design.

CONTENTS

The Lord Is My Shepherd

PSALM 23:1–6, A PSALM OF DAVID

The LORD is my shepherd; I shall not want.

He maketh me to lie down in green pastures:
he leadeth me beside the still waters.

He restoreth my soul:
he leadeth me in the paths of righteousness
for his name's sake.

Yea, though I walk through
the valley of the shadow of death,
I will fear no evil: for thou art with me;
thy rod and thy staff they comfort me.

Thou preparest a table before me
in the presence of mine enemies:
thou anointest my head with oil;
my cup runneth over.

Surely goodness and mercy shall
follow me all the days of my life: and
I will dwell in the house of the LORD forever.

CHAPTER ONE

March 1990: The Journey Begins

"We need to talk." With these words from our daughter's surgeon, our world turned upside down in a microsecond. The doctor went on to tell us that our daughter, Rachelle, thirteen years of age, had a malignant mass in her abdomen, larger than they had ever seen before. She weighed only ninety pounds and was barely five feet tall, but they estimated that at least thirty pounds of that were cancerous tumors on every organ in her abdomen. With tears in his eyes, the doctor said that the entire surgical team was crying as they worked. He personally felt there was no hope but was committed to giving us some options. My husband and I looked at each other, overcome with shock and heartbreak, trying to hold back tears while struggling to make immediate, life-changing decisions.

As some background to acquaint you with us, we are a family of five: myself, my husband, Jamie; our daughter, Rachelle; our son, Jason (age twelve at this time); and our youngest son, Joshua (age four). Each one of our family members is a born-again Christian. We believe in building our family with Bible principles, faith in what Christ has done for us, and Bible-based Christian values.

At the time of these events, we were living in Evanston, Wyoming, where my husband pastored Uinta Bible Baptist Church. Originally from Texas, our family had moved to Wyoming specifically because we wanted to minister in the northwest United States. We had long held a heart for establishing churches in areas where Bible-preaching Baptist churches are in short supply. We loved Wyoming; it felt like home to us, even though we had no other biological family in the area.

At that time, Evanston was a city of about ten thousand people with an economy strongly based in the oil and gas industry. The church in Evanston had been through some tough times financially and many of the members had been transferred out of state due to a recent oil bust. Although the church was running with only about sixteen people in attendance, including our family, when we moved there, the members were excited and welcomed us. However, because the financial constraints were more than we expected, we considered the possibility of whether we should stay. After much prayer, we believed the Lord gave us the verse from Ephesians 6:13, and my husband and I committed to *"having done all to stand."* We knew God wanted us to do all we could and to simply stand in place. That would require both Jamie and me working secondary jobs in order to supplement our income. I worked part-time for a few months at the local hospital and then was hired as an assistant in administration for the county school district. This was a job-share position, which was a wonderful blessing, as I worked flexible, part-time hours yet had full benefits. Jamie started driving a bus for the county school district, which was also a blessing, as the part-time hours enabled him to still juggle the responsibilities of the pastorate. These jobs also helped us become acquainted with Evanston, opening doors for positive interactions and building relationships within the community.

We had lived there only eighteen months when our daughter was given the cancer diagnosis in March 1990. Six months before, we had taken her to our family doctor because she was exhibiting fatigue that was unusual for her age. She seemed extremely tired all the time, and even when she had her friends over to our house to visit, she would go straight to bed. The doctor ran tests and even looked for leukemia, but nothing showed up in the lab work. While waiting for these results, I remember being very concerned. Feeling anxious and sick at heart, I caught myself repeatedly praying, "God, please don't let her die!" When the test reports came back and the doctor told us that everything was clear with no evident need for concern, I felt a little silly for overreacting. Then, things began to change.

On Sunday, March 11, 1990, Rachelle stayed home from church with an upset stomach. That evening, Jason and Joshua also were sick, so all three stayed home from church services. Because the church was next door to our home, and I was the church pianist, I went back and forth throughout the church service to check on them. That evening, when I took Rachelle's temperature, I noticed that her stomach looked much more swollen than before, although she was now running no fever. Without expressing my concern to her, I simply told Rachelle that I was going to take her to the doctor on Monday to get checked. First thing Monday morning, I called and set her an appointment for the afternoon. She and the boys were feeling better with the stomach complaints; in fact, later that morning, Rachelle called and told me that she did not want to go to the doctor because she was feeling better. With the appointment already set and a sense of urgency in my heart, I insisted that we go anyway. Like puzzle pieces coming together, I started making connections that made me heartsick again. She had also been complaining for about a week of a pain in her shoulder that pain relievers did not seem to help. In addition, about three weeks before, she had come to me, somewhat concerned, and showed me a lump on her abdomen. Because there was no pain, and the recent tests seemed to be good, I dismissed it and said we would just watch it.

This time when her doctor examined her, we knew immediately from his countenance that something was terribly wrong. At one point, he actually looked at Rachelle and asked her if she was pregnant. My innocent thirteen-year-old was horrified—and me too! Upon hearing her resounding NO, he then told us that she was either three months pregnant or there was a huge tumor in her abdomen. He started making preparations to send us to the local hospital for tests, with the possibility of doing emergency surgery that night. As we walked over to the lab, I remember praying as we walked: "Lord, what should I pray for? Either of these options, pregnancy or cancer, is devastating!" There was no reason to suspect pregnancy; she had no boyfriend, nor physical contact or opportunity. While she was having blood drawn in the lab, I called Jamie and told him what was transpiring. The tests were, of course, negative on the pregnancy. We could not proceed with the necessary CAT scan, however, because she needed an enema prep first, so we were sent home to drink the liquid contrast and do the enema in preparation for the CAT scan first thing the next morning (Tuesday).

Naturally, that night we were all anxious. Jamie and I prayed together, talked, and decided that we would take her to Salt Lake City to Primary Children's Hospital for any surgery that was recommended. That night, none of us could sleep. Rachelle lay on the living room couch all night, and I lay on the floor next to her. I listened to her struggle to breathe, not yet knowing that the shoulder pain of which she had been complaining was caused by her lungs filling up with fluid from the cancer.

Tuesday morning we went for scans at the local Evanston hospital. Several church friends joined us there to await the results. We were sitting in the waiting room when the doctor walked in the door. His face was very grave as he informed us that it was a large lymphoma.

I said, "What is that? I don't remember."

He explained, "It is cancer of the lymph nodes."

I reacted, "But that's highly fatal!"

He looked me in the eye and sadly replied, "Yes." He then went on to explain that she needed surgery right away and that he was making arrangements to send us to the Primary Children's Hospital in Salt Lake City, about eighty miles away, for surgery tentatively scheduled for that very afternoon.

When the doctor left the room, I felt completely numb. I excused myself and went to the hospital bathroom, seeking some needed privacy. Once there, I knelt at the sink, crying out to God, "She's Yours! I gave her to You at birth. She's Yours to take. But Lord, help me—it's too hard!"

A few minutes later, a worried fellow church member checked on me. When she stepped inside, I was still on the floor, crying and saying, "She belongs to God, and He has a right to take her." Exiting the bathroom, we ran into another church member. I tried to keep myself composed for Rachelle's sake. As we walked back down the hall, I saw Rachelle coming toward us, and I almost fell apart completely. I turned around to get a drink at the water fountain, attempting to keep Rachelle from seeing me crying.

I said to the ladies, "How can I tell her she's going to die?" I almost collapsed but felt as though God's hand lifted me up. We all went together, Rachelle, Jamie, and our church friends, to look at the CAT scan results and talk to the doctors. That is when Rachelle saw the tumor for the first time as well. All we could see in her abdomen was one giant mass. Every organ was covered with what the doctors estimated as thirty

✦✦✦

Once there, I knelt at the sink, crying out to God, "She's Yours! I gave her to You at birth. She's Yours to take. But Lord, help me—it's too hard!"

✦✦✦

pounds of cancerous tumors. Rachelle has always been small, and she weighed only about ninety pounds at the time, which now overwhelmed us with the realization that one-third of her body weight was cancer.

Immediately, we needed to make the eighty-mile trip to Salt Lake City's Primary Children's Hospital. Hurriedly, we made arrangements with our jobs and for our boys to stay with church families.

✦✦✦

PSALM 119:175–176

Let my soul live, and it shall praise thee;
and let thy judgments help me.
I have gone astray like a lost sheep; seek thy servant;
for I do not forget thy commandments.

CHAPTER TWO

My Innocent Lamb

Once we arrived at Primary Children's Hospital on Tuesday afternoon, we were disappointed with the crowded condition of the hospital and the seemingly slow and tedious chore of checking in and then seeing doctors. The surgeon's office kept us waiting for what seemed like an eternity, as they were dealing with a baby who was critically ill with a Wilmes' tumor. The baby's family was understandably distraught. We realized that we were not the only family facing the challenges and heartbreak of a child fighting for life.

Finally, we were put into a patient room, but it was on the infant floor with very young babies all around, and we had to share a room. We learned then that the hospital conditions were due to it being a very busy, overcrowded, and overextended teaching hospital that was actively in transition and trying to move to a new, larger facility in the near future. The hospital personnel were wonderful and doing their best to make the difficult circumstances as comfortable as possible for patients and families alike.

The surgery schedule was full, so Rachelle's surgery was postponed until Wednesday and then eventually Thursday. The waiting and uncertainty were agonizing for us all. The surgical resident came in to visit us, then the surgeon and his team. They tried to reassure us and told us that they felt sure that her tumor was Meigs syndrome, a benign tumor that occasionally presents itself in girls this age. We were elated at the possibility of it being Meigs syndrome rather than cancer.

Up until that time, my emotions were extremely raw. I was smiling on the outside yet would see my reflection in the mirror with tears running down my cheeks. I could not calmly or rationally verbalize a prayer. Rather, it seemed I was constantly yelling in my heart, "Please, please, please, God!"

Wednesday we spent the day doing her heart workup in preparation for surgery. Rachelle had been diagnosed with a heart condition ten years earlier, an irregular heartbeat, now called SVT (supraventricular tachycardia). The workup revealed that this condition had become more severe and would now have to be controlled with medicine, in comparison to her earlier diagnosis that it could just "run its course." The cardiologist gave directions that she was to be sent straight to the emergency room if the rapid heartbeats started without stopping right away. Again, the surgeons seemed sure there was no hurry to schedule Rachelle's surgery, as they believed it was a benign tumor. Our family doctor drove down to see us from Evanston and reacted with shocked disagreement when we told him of this diagnosis. However, we were determined to be optimistic and believe the best.

We became acquainted with the mother of our hospital roommate and learned that this baby had a serious neurological problem as well as a brother with leukemia. This served, again, as a needed reminder to us that we are never alone in our trials and sorrows, as many other people in the world are also hurting. The mother was friendly, and we had a nice visit.

Rachelle did not talk much. She did not want to talk about anything, including her illness. Truthfully, she was terrified at the complete disintegration of her thirteen-year-old world. Emotionally, she wrestled with being resentful, short-tempered, and simply scared.

On Wednesday afternoon, we were blessed and surprised when pastors from other independent Baptist churches in the area heard our news and came to the hospital. They stood around Rachelle's hospital bed, anointed her with oil, and prayed over her for healing. It was very moving, and although this was a new experience for us, I could tell Rachelle was appreciative, and we were encouraged.

Finally, early Thursday, they took her to surgery. Our fear seemed tangible, almost overwhelming; we were all so frightened. A local pastor and his wife came to be with us, and we prayed together. We were allowed to walk down the hallway to the elevator with Rachelle as they wheeled her bed to the surgical room. Telling her goodbye, we walked to the waiting room. During that time, we tried to make small talk and pass what we knew would be a long wait. Suddenly, I felt compelled to walk down the hall and go into the hospital bathroom for some privacy to pray. While I was in there, I heard the Lord speak to me. Not audibly, but very clearly in my heart. I knew it was His voice.

I felt the Lord say to me, "Vickie, do you remember what her name is?"

I responded, "Well yes, Lord. It's Rachelle."

Then He asked me, "Do you know what it means?"

"No, not really," I replied. "You know we just named her that at the last minute because I thought it was pretty."

God replied, "It means innocent lamb. I want you to remember what my Innocent Lamb did. He died. He did not deserve it. He died that others might live. This is for My glory."

I began to sob uncontrollably as I absolutely knew that God was speaking to me, telling me that Rachelle had cancer and warning me of the outcome. I believed He was telling me that as Christ had died, so Rachelle would die. I know He wanted me to know it was for His purpose, not as a punishment to our family or me.

I want to say here that we have learned that trials can be for different reasons. They can be a discipline or they may be a natural consequence of our own decisions and behaviors. However, trials can also come to us simply that God may get the glory for it, and I believe that God wanted me to know this.

✦✦✦

Trials can come to us simply that God may get the glory for it.

✦✦✦

When I went back to the waiting room and sat down, I was too embarrassed and overwhelmed to say anything, yet I felt strongly compelled that I should share what had happened. Finally, I told the visiting pastor's wife, but I was still not sure how to tell Jamie. I was afraid he would think I was having a mental breakdown from the overwhelming stress.

Shortly after, and much sooner than we expected, the doctor came to the door and said, "We need to talk." I felt myself walk as if in a dream as we tried to find someplace to talk privately. The hospital renovation and transition gave little options for this. We finally ended up on the infant floor in the playroom and sat down in small baby chairs at a children's table. We knew from his demeanor what the doctor was going to say.

He then proceeded to tell us that Rachelle was in the advanced stages of non-Hodgkin's lymphoma cancer. He told us that it was a huge tumor and completely inoperable. It appeared to have begun on her appendix and then spread throughout all her abdominal organs, completely up to and including her diaphragm. The surgical team was performing a bone marrow biopsy as we spoke. They were also removing one of her ovaries (we had already signed permission for it to be removed in anticipation of Meigs syndrome) for biopsy purposes as well as her abdominal flap. The surgical team would be attempting to look around the abdomen, push the tumor back in, and close her up. He told us that the one ovary to be removed was a cancerous mass that weighed three pounds and that the other ovary was a three-pound tumor as well.

In addition to the estimated thirty pounds of tumor, her heart was also enlarged, and her lungs were filling with fluid. I asked the doctor in desperation, "Why didn't you take it out?" meaning all the cancerous tumor.

He looked at me and replied, "We will have to literally cut her in half to get it all." Even to start removing some of it was dangerous, because she could bleed to death, and he believed it was useless to do that anyway. He told us that they had not seen anything like it before, and the members of the surgical team were crying as they worked. Although the doctor did not expect her to survive, he assured us that the oncology team would work with us, if that was what we chose to do. We had serious decisions to make and quickly. Would we take her home and let her die quietly, or would we start the cancer treatments, even though, to the surgeon's knowledge, no child had survived this? If we did choose to start chemotherapy treatment, he explained, she would need a heart catheter inserted immediately, while she was still opened up in surgery, and had us sign a consent form. Jamie and I looked at each other and decided we would fight this cancer. We would pursue the chemotherapy treatment, believing that where there is life, there is hope.

The doctor left us to rejoin Rachelle's surgical team, after explaining that she would be placed in the ICU when they completed the surgery and that the oncology team would be down to see us. He also told us that we needed to talk to the finance office right away. This was going to be a very expensive endeavor.

I remember reacting in my heart by questioning, "Doesn't God love her?" and yet knowing absolutely that He did. We went back into Rachelle's hospital room with our friends and started making phone calls to our parents. We simply told them what the doctor said and then hung up the phone because there was nothing more to say. God's presence was there, tangible, as though His arms were around us. Various friends and church members came to comfort and encourage us. We ended up standing in a circle and praying. We decided to go get something to eat because we knew Rachelle would be in recovery for some time before she would be placed in the ICU, and we had had nothing to eat all day. Also, we had to move out of her current hospital room because she was now being admitted as an ICU patient.

We carried our personal things over to a room we were renting from the hospital for ten dollars a night and then went for hamburgers. While we talked, we decided it would be best for Jamie to ride back home to Evanston with friends so that I would have a car. Also, he needed to be able to talk to Jason (age twelve) and Joshua (age four) before others did, to break the news and to try to give them some stability. Our entire family was in this journey together. Jamie and I decided that I would focus on Rachelle, and he would focus on the boys and the church. When we got back to the hospital, Rachelle had already been moved to the ICU, so we went right in to see her, although she was barely conscious. Then Jamie returned home, and I settled into the hospital.

It was not until the pediatric oncologist tested and reviewed the biopsy that we were given any hope at all for her survival. The oncologist told us that this type of cancer had been responding to chemotherapy in about 50 to 60 percent of the cases nationwide. Rachelle's cancer was level three out of four. It had not spread into her spinal fluid or bone marrow, which was cause for some optimism. However, the chemo had to be started immediately, as the tumor was doubling in size daily. So the next day after this major abdominal surgery, Rachelle was started on a very aggressive six-drug chemotherapy regimen. This chemo regimen was so toxic that I was told that one-third of the children given this treatment die from the chemo itself. Another time we were told she had only a 40 percent chance of surviving the treatment alone (not regarding the cancer). Her protocol was that she had a chemo treatment every two weeks. One included a spinal tap with chemo administered into her spine (we called this the *big* one, because it made her very sick). The second one was longer (four hours to administer one of the drugs) but easier on her physically, therefore, we called it the *little* one. She was assigned a projected eighteen-month protocol for the chemo treatments.

Emotionally drained, we felt our family would never be the same. After Rachelle's surgery, my husband and I looked at each other, and I said, "You know, we're going to have to decide right now that we're not going to let this destroy our marriage." Our experience had shown us that challenges like this often end in divorce. We discussed that we were going to have to work together and not against each other and vowed again to stand together. We have a marriage verse from Ecclesiastes 4:12, *"and a threefold chord is not quickly broken."* This was engraved in our wedding bands and reminded us that our threefold chord was made up of the two of us and God. This commitment was a good thing for us, but there were times in this journey that we had to stop and remember our vows and to look at what we were doing. We felt the best way to deal with Rachelle's long-term illness was, again, for me to stay with her in the hospital and to deal with the doctors, medicines and her illness and to just be her support system. Jamie would focus on home, the boys, and their schedules, trying to keep their lives as normal as possible while working to keep the church and ministry stable.

Rachelle was to be in the hospital about two more weeks. As mentioned already, when they brought Rachelle into the recovery room where we could be with her, she was barely conscious. However, the next day, she woke for a moment, looked directly at me, and said, "Mom, is it bad? Is it cancer?" Oh how I wanted to lie to her! But I knew I shouldn't.

I said quietly, "Rachelle, it is cancer." She started crying. I said over and over, "But it's going to be fine. It's going to be OK." Honestly, I did not think I was speaking truth, but I also did not want her to give up. (Praise God, He knew it was truth!) Despite the overcrowded hospital, she was moved into a private ICU room because there was so much going on with her and also because of interest in her medical case. Teams of doctors would look through the window at her, then would come into the room and talk about her case. She hated all the attention and discussion going on around her and tried to ignore them. I was very glad that I had already told her it was cancer because she certainly would have ascertained that from these conversations.

Because she was in the ICU, I could not stay overnight with her in her room, so the hospital arranged for me to stay in a room across the street. Rachelle was still mostly sleeping from the surgery, Jamie had left to go back home, and I badly needed sleep. I went to the room to sleep a few hours but asked for medical staff to contact me when she had her first chemo treatment, scheduled to begin in the middle of that very night. Having heard the horror stories of chemotherapy treatment, no one seemed to know what to expect, and I wanted to be with her during the treatment.

Right on schedule, in the middle of the night, a knock came at my door. I woke up, got up to answer it, opened the door, and then proceeded to faint away onto the floor. The messenger who came to tell me that the chemo treatment was beginning ended up reviving me and telling me I had to go back to bed. I did. I was completely at the end of myself physically and emotionally. The next morning, when I went back to Rachelle's room, the nurses told me that she had done well with the chemo, and they had kept a close eye on her. We rejoiced that she did not get sick. With an eighteen-inch incision running the entire length of her abdomen, the vomiting that often resulted would have been intolerable.

Two days later, Rachelle was moved from the ICU to a regular room, then again to another one. Due to the hospital transition and overcrowding, every room had multiple children and parents trying to squeeze into every inch of space. Even to get a chair in which to sit was like a grand prize. Several of the medical staff tried to get Rachelle to walk, but she was in so much pain, and so upset about the whole situation, that she flatly refused. When she was assigned to another room, we tricked her and told her she had to walk to get to her room. She did, but when she realized it was a trick, she was angry with me the rest of the day. However, she did start walking then.

For me, the stress and fatigue triggered a massive migraine that was so severe that I experienced some seizure-like activity with it. This can be normal for me; however, it frightened the nurses so badly that, before I knew it, an ambulance crew was coming to get me from Rachelle's room. They transported me to another hospital because I could not be treated at a pediatric hospital. Thankfully, after examining me, they took me back to Rachelle, but it was frightening for both of us.

After a few days, my parents came up from Texas, and my mother was able to stay with Rachelle to give me a break from the hospital as we continued to stay in Salt Lake City. My birthday fell during this hospital stay, so Jamie came and took me out to eat at my favorite restaurant there.

Another day, when a friend came and said she would stay with Rachelle, I headed for a Christian bookstore. This was a terrible trial to face, that our daughter was dying. I did not really know how to deal with this. I have always loved to read, so I rationalized that surely there was a book I could pick up that would give me "ten steps to deal with a dying child." At that time in Salt Lake City, there was only one small Christian bookstore in the area. I drove there and walked in the front door and straight to the register where I could ask for help finding such a book. Right in front of my eyes, on the center display, was a calligraphy plaque with the name RACHELLE on it and under it was written *innocent lamb*. I had never seen her name on anything. I immediately knew this was a sign from the Lord, as He was reminding me again that this was for His glory! So I bought the plaque instead of a book, and we hung it over her bed in the hospital. We were in a great trial, but God was reminding me that He was in charge. But God was not done yet with the trials.

•••

PSALM 40:11–12

Withhold not thou thy tender mercies from me, O Lord:
let thy lovingkindness and thy truth continually preserve me.

For innumerable evils have compassed me about:
mine iniquities have taken hold upon me,
so that I am not able to look up; they are more than
the hairs of mine head: therefore my heart faileth me.

CHAPTER THREE

April 1990: The Trials Continue

In early April, we were able to take Rachelle home from the hospital and back to Evanston. She had been home only a few days when she began screaming in pain. I looked up one morning to see her running through the house screaming hysterically and completely out of her mind because the pain was so intense. Our regular local doctor was out of town, but when I called the office, the doctor's assistant reassured me that things would be fine, and they made an appointment for later that morning. They thought it was abdominal cramping that was a natural result of her extensive surgery. Because I had missed so much work, I decided to go in to my job for a while and try to catch up while Jamie took Rachelle to the doctor.

Although this was early April, Evanston is at seven-thousand-foot elevation, and a late snowstorm was underway. It was not unheard of for snow to fall every month of the year in Evanston. (In fact, during one Fourth of July celebration on our church property, the children were shooting fireworks in the snow, and the parents were sitting in their pickups drinking hot chocolate!)

Now with another snowstorm going full blast, Jamie began driving Rachelle to the doctor in our Ford minivan. They hit a patch of ice and lost control of the van. It rolled on its side dangerously close to the edge of a twenty-foot dropoff. Both Jamie and Rachelle were left hanging upside down by their seat belts.

Jamie remembers looking down at Rachelle as she looked back up to him, her facial expression saying, "Dad, what else can go wrong?" A passerby (the mayor of Evanston) stopped, helped them get out of the vehicle, and took them to the emergency room. Jamie was standing there in the emergency room with Rachelle when his boss from the transportation department came in looking for him. He had seen the van rolled on the side of the road and recognized it as ours. As his supervisor walked into the examination room, Jamie turned, wrapped his arms around him, and wept uncontrollably on his shoulder. Jamie was overwhelmed with the thought, *Here's my daughter, dying of cancer, and now I almost killed her in a car wreck!*

I received a phone call at my desk and was informed of the accident. I literally had an emotional shut-down. I could not think straight; I could not digest what I had been told. I simply thanked whoever called and went back to work as though nothing had happened. Fortunately, a co-worker in the room overheard the conversation, recognized what was happening, and talked to me, encouraging me to go to the hospital. It was as though a light came on, and I rushed to the hospital to find that Jamie was uninjured but that Rachelle had been admitted. Her injuries from the accident were not serious, but she had been hanging by the seatbelt across her abdomen, only a few weeks after a major surgery that was already complicated by the fact that her surgical incision was not healing. We learned that chemotherapy can interfere with healing, so we were now also dealing with dehiscing, a potentially serious complication.

After Rachelle was found to have no specific injuries from the accident, we also needed to determine what was causing her intense abdominal pain that had initiated the trip to the doctor in the first place. Again, the doctor's assistant said there was no major problem, and with pain medication, she seemed to be better, although she was admitted into the hospital for observation.

Jamie left to prepare for Wednesday night prayer meeting at the church. With the latest events heavy on his heart, he found himself looking out the church windows in reflection as church members began to drive into the parking lot. One of the men entered into the auditorium, walked up to him and said, "Preacher, you must have a lot of sin in your life for all these things to be happening to you."

My husband was completely shocked by this accusation and the realization that these trials were a poor reflection on his testimony as a believer. He also could not bear the thought that his daughter could be suffering all these things because of some sin in his life. After a few seconds, he was able to calmly respond reassuringly to the church member. This gave us another reminder that words can help or they can hurt.

This gave us another reminder that words can help or they can hurt.

In the meantime, our son Jason had been competing successfully in spelling bees and now was scheduled to be in the state spelling bee within a few days. Because this was important to Jason, and Rachelle appeared to be stable, my husband left to drive Jason and two other contestants across the state to the competition in Lander, Wyoming.

After they left, however, Rachelle's pain intensified, and her regular doctor came in, checked her out, and sadly informed me that she was actually very critically ill. They had discovered she had a complication from her recent surgery and had developed a serious bowel obstruction, or "kink" in the bowel, which was a life-threatening situation. Immediately, I made quick arrangements for Joshua to stay with a babysitter in Evanston, as Rachelle and I were loaded into an ambulance to be driven back to Salt Lake City's Primary Children's Hospital.

After examining Rachelle there, her doctors informed me that this complication would take her life within hours if it did not resolve itself, and they recommended emergency surgery. However, they also told me that the chances of her surviving the surgery itself were small and further complicated by the cancer and the effects of the chemotherapy treatment. I had to make the decision whether to give consent for them to operate or not. My daughter was crying in unbearable pain, and the doctors were looking to me for an answer. I had no peace about the surgery! *Perhaps it would resolve itself,* I frantically thought.

I could not reach my husband, even to let him know about the crisis, let alone to ask for his guidance. I begged the doctors for time, and they reluctantly agreed. Throughout the night, doctors would come to me every hour on the hour to check on Rachelle and to see what I wanted to do, if I was ready to sign the consent for the surgery. I felt as though I were being asked to sign her death warrant. I spent the entire night standing next to her bed, praying and massaging her head and singing hymns softly to her without a break. If I stopped for even a minute, she would beg me to continue, as the singing and the words helped her endure the agony. I sang every hymn I could think of. Eventually, I lost my voice and was hoarsely croaking in her ear, but she would not let me stop.

Once again the doctor came in around 4:00 a.m., and this time he firmly said to me, "It is not resolving itself. We must operate immediately!" I begged him for just one more hour as I prayed and sang. During that hour, I sensed the angel of God was giving us strength, and I submitted to God's will and leadership. When the doctor returned, I was finally prepared to sign the consent for surgery. He checked her once again, then looked at me in disbelief and said, "It's resolving itself! I think she's going to be all right without the surgery." An amazing answer to prayer! There have been times without number that I felt God's presence and knew angels were around us, watching with us and over us. Although it was agonizing to be awake all night and to watch one I love suffer so much, I knew I was not alone. Now Rachelle and I watched the dawn break with new hope. It was not the last battle for her life, but God had again, faithfully walked us through it.

✦✦✦

PSALM 40:16–17

Let all those that seek thee rejoice and be glad in thee;
let such as love thy salvation say continually,
the LORD *be magnified.*

But I am poor and needy;
yet the LORD *thinketh upon me:*
thou art my help and my deliverer;
make no tarrying, O my God.

CHAPTER FOUR

Easter 1990: What Else Can Go Wrong?

We quickly learned not to ask, "What else can go wrong?" Within a few weeks, I was driving Rachelle and Joshua to school one morning, again on icy roads, when a driver made a sudden U-turn in the road in front of me. Trying to avert an accident with this car, I lost control of my vehicle, hitting that car and ending up stopped in the middle of the road. I stepped out of our vehicle to check on the other driver when another car topped the hill, slamming on their brakes when they saw the accident ahead. Again, the icy conditions took over as they also lost control and crashed into our vehicle with our children still inside. For a moment, I thought I was watching two of my children be killed at once! By God's amazing grace, no one was seriously injured, but our car was a total loss and we were financially unable to replace it. We had a second car, a twenty-year-old clunker, as a back-up that we barely trusted to get us across town, but it now became our transportation for the bi-monthly trips to Salt Lake City.

April was passing quickly, and Easter weekend was approaching. We had already scheduled a week-long trip to Denver to spend with friends and to keep an appointment for myself with a doctor who specialized in Meniere's disease. I had been diagnosed several years earlier and had undergone two ear surgeries in an effort to address the degeneration of my hearing as well as my balance problems. Having learned of this specialist in Denver, I had made an appointment with him to coincide with the planned trip to see friends, but that was before we learned Rachelle's diagnosis. We decided to keep the appointment in Denver and see what the doctor recommended for me. During my visit, I was very impressed with the doctor's knowledge and suggestions but was taken aback when he said I had a pinched blood vessel in my brain that was causing much of my problems. He recommended that I undergo brain surgery, a vascular loop decompression for the condition. The idea of dealing with brain surgery on top of Rachelle's health seemed overwhelming, and I could not think of undergoing it immediately; however, I scheduled it for six months later. I rationalized that maybe the brain surgery would help me to be more physically able to help Rachelle through her cancer journey.

While we were visiting in Denver those first couple of days, Rachelle's hair seemed to be thinning slightly. The oncologists had warned us that she would lose her hair, but Rachelle, as a strong-minded thirteen-year-old, decided that could not be tolerated, so she determined that she simply was not going to lose her hair. After all, the doctors had said there "probably" would be hair loss, not "definitely." I tried to talk to her about wigs, but she would not even discuss it. Without telling her, I finally went alone and bought a wig similar to her current hair-style that I thought would work, just in case.

Easter morning came, and we got up to get ready to go to Sunday school with our friends. As Rachelle was getting ready in the bathroom, we suddenly heard a frantic yell, "MOM!" Jamie and I both went running to the bathroom, and when we opened the door, all we could see was hair. Hair was everywhere, floating in the air and covering the floor and the fixtures. It looked like someone had blown a truckload of hair into the small room. Her hair had come out, all right, and all at once. She was completely devastated. That seemed to be one of those times when she had lost all hope. The rest of the family and our friends went on to Sunday school to celebrate Resurrection Sunday while Rachelle and I stayed back to work through this.

After a little time, when she was calmer, I pulled out the wig and showed it to her. She tried it on, over her now bald head, and she actually liked it and brightened up a bit. We went on to the morning worship service with her "new look." She liked the wig so much that she would hardly take it off. It seemed to almost become her security blanket. She wore it so much for the next several months that it became pretty ragged looking, and I had to finally talk her into discarding it and getting another one. Only one time during the entire illness did Rachelle let her dad see her bald head.

PSALM 77:1–14

TO THE CHIEF MUSICIAN, TO JEDUTHUN
A PSALM OF ASAPH

I cried unto God with my voice,
even unto God with my voice;
and he gave ear unto me.

In the day of my trouble I sought the Lord:
my sore ran in the night, and ceased not:
my soul refused to be comforted.

I remembered God, and was troubled:
I complained, and my spirit was overwhelmed.
Selah.

Thou holdest mine eyes waking:
I am so troubled that I cannot speak.

I have considered the days of old,
the years of ancient times.

I call to remembrance my song in the night:
I commune with mine own heart:
and my spirit made diligent search.

Will the Lord cast off forever?
and will he be favourable no more?

Is his mercy clean gone forever?
doth his promise fail for evermore?

Hath God forgotten to be gracious?
hath he in anger shut up his tender mercies?
Selah.

And I said, This is my infirmity:
but I will remember the years of the
right hand of the most High.

I will remember the works of the Lord:
surely I will remember thy wonders of old.

I will meditate also of all thy work,
and talk of thy doings.

Thy way, O God, is in the sanctuary:
who is so great a God as our God?

Thou art the God that doest wonders:
thou hast declared thy strength among the people.

CHAPTER FIVE

The Sheep Respond

How did we individually handle all this? Let me share some of the challenges we each faced.

My feelings at first when talking to the doctor were a mixture of horror and detachment. *This cannot really be happening.* After a while, it turned into grieving; I would catch myself trying to smile, yet tears would be flowing. Every thought was something like, *Well, this is the last time I'll see Rachelle do such and such,* or *I'll never get to do that with Rachelle again.* I even regretfully thought of all the money wasted on Rachelle's piano lessons. One night, talking to a friend, I heard myself sounding as though there was no hope. "I bet you're grateful to have your two girls, all healthy, and here I probably won't have a daughter next year." I still remember the pain in her countenance as I wallowed in a conversation of self-pity. I acted and talked almost as though

Rachelle were already dead. Suddenly it was as though I heard myself from outside, as I was saying things like that. The Lord smote my heart. *Where was my faith? Where was my focus? Where was my hope?* Right then I determined not to waste anymore of her life grieving. If she died, I could grieve then, but not while she was still alive and fighting for her life. I chose to be grateful for each day of life and to count every single blessing God gave in the journey. This was a game changer for me.

Jamie, on the other hand, dealt with his emotions mainly by laughing, joking, and keeping things light. We discovered that finding things to laugh about really helped. Often nurses and friends would comment about our smiles and humor.

Jamie had some problems with denial. We have learned that denial can be a coping response for some going through trials. At first he told several people that her cancer was no problem; it was the easiest cancer to cure. I believe that when the doctors told us, in fact, that her cancer was difficult to cure and that she was in an advanced stage, he could not cope and actually believed what he wanted to hear. Sometimes in the treatment process, when she suffered from extreme fatigue, mouth sores, and headaches, if she complained, he would almost shut down and not believe her. It was as though he could not accept that his precious only daughter could be going through this horrible experience.

♦♦♦

I chose to be grateful for each day of life and to count every single blessing God gave in the journey.

♦♦♦

When he did allow himself to think of her potential death, he was bound by fear. He woke up one morning, sat up in the middle of our bed, and decided it was time to deal with the reality of the situation. He began to make plans for Rachelle's funeral. We even purchased a burial plot in our hometown in Texas, just to be prepared.

Jamie was a wonderful dad in this journey. He would sit up all night with Rachelle while she was vomiting violently, would clean things up, and would be very patient and loving with her. When the vomiting would slow down and she felt like she could try to eat something, he would make trips into town to buy her whatever she thought sounded good—burritos or pizza rolls. Jamie was the glue that held our family together. He was determined to be strong and to keep us going forward, and he did a great job of it.

Jason, at twelve years of age, was in a very trying transitional time, his first year of middle school. He grew four inches taller during the first few months of Rachelle's treatment. To have the family so disrupted was almost more than he could cope with. He had to learn to act responsibly and to react maturely in a hurry. We needed him to help with things, such as watching Joshua and helping with dishes, whereas in the past, Rachelle had always helped and watched the boys. He was resentful, at times, of the change to our lives and of Rachelle getting so much attention. There were even occasions when he would fight with her and tell her he hoped she died. We tried to take extra pains to give him love and attention and to do special things with him when we could. Thankfully, this hard time was short lived. He really did the maturing he needed to do, felt better emotionally about the situation, and became just a great person. By age thirteen, we described him in our Christmas letter as follows: "He is a joy to be around at age thirteen (I'm not kidding!) and is involved in everything he can be. In addition to spelling bee competitions, he makes straight A's, has been on the student council this year, is an All-Star in baseball, a running-back on the football team, and is now a forward on the basketball team. Our only complaint is not seeing him very much!"

Jason wrote about his experience and submitted an article to Focus on the Family's Christian teen magazine, *Breakaway*, published in the summer of 1990.

> *My dad's been a Baptist pastor for ten years. He's loving and cares about other people's problems and feelings. He's always supporting me and encouraging me in everything I do. Just recently, my fourteen-year-old sister was diagnosed with cancer. I didn't know what to do. But there was Dad. He kept pushing my brother and me to keep praying and assured us everything would be all right… I didn't feel depressed, and he helped me to have more confidence. Now my sister is much better. Every other week she has a chemotherapy treatment. My dad is always there to hold her hand or comfort her when she's sick. The past year I was in the state spelling bee. (It was about the time my sister got sick.) Well, my dad drove me and two other girls to it, two hundred miles away, even though my sister was in the hospital recovering from surgery.*

Jason won second place in this writing competition and was awarded several baseball cards and a baseball personally autographed by Orel Hershiser, which really thrilled Jason's heart.

Joshua, at four years old, also had a hard time with the adjustments. He suddenly was staying with babysitters more than usual and even spending nights with them, after having spent very little time with sitters previously. He would cry a lot and be afraid of us leaving him, struggling with fear and insecurity. One of the sitters became very upset with him the night that Rachelle was critically ill with the bowel blockage. She told me later that "he cried so much that I had to lock him up in the basement and made him stay there alone all night to punish him." We obviously needed to find some other childcare provider for him. We tried another provider, only to discover that she let him watch the movie *Killer Clowns from Outer Space*. As a four-year-old, the trauma from this movie stayed with him for years. He still does not like clowns. This simply did not work. We put him into the city daycare, but he ran away from there twice. Even when he started kindergarten, he spent the first two days crying and being "held down" so that he would not run away. Faced with the challenge of finding a suitable sitter for him, we finally re-adjusted our schedules go that he could be with either parent whenever he was out of school. If needed, for a short time, our assistant pastor would also watch him at the church, and this worked very well. Actually, they seemed to both enjoy the fun. This gave him some stability and he seemed to come out of his insecurity, and it gave us the opportunity to give him more attention as he matured and adjusted. By the time he turned five, we would often describe him as "lots of fun and usually keeping us laughing!"

These times were also a challenge on our marriage. I became so involved with Rachelle's healthcare that it became my main emphasis in life. I had to keep track of communications with multiple doctors, medications, schedules, and treatment for complications from the chemo. I was her advocate, and I would fight for what was important to her. I provided her with the necessary homecare for the Broviac line that ran from her chest into her heart. This had to be cleaned and changed daily while in a very sterile environment. In the hospital, I was the only person she would allow to go in with her, holding her hand, during the excruciatingly painful spinal taps.

There were times when we would be away from home for days, and Jamie would call to talk and spend some time with me, but I would devote the whole conversation telling him things I needed him to do while I was gone. As mentioned earlier, Jamie's responsibility fell to staying at home in Evanston, taking care of the boys and the church ministry and working as a part-time school bus driver. There were times he struggled with resentment of that, as he needed to get some attention from me, and rightfully so. It sometimes felt that everything in our family was centered around hospitals and doctors. We each struggled with times of feeling neglected, mistreated, and resentful.

How did Rachelle react? At first, she was angry and resentful. She was occasionally rude to the nurses, telling them they weren't doing things right or how she liked the other nurse better, things of that nature. She was not used to being sick at all, much less laying around in pain and knowing her world was being turned upside down. As time went by, however, she matured and accepted the situation. She decided this was strictly a temporary situation that was not going to get her down. Determined to be optimistic, she never missed school if there was any way she could crawl out of bed and get there. She was adamant about keeping her grades up, even with missing a few days of school every other week. She would not talk much about her illness, as that seemed to her to be admitting defeat. However, on the spinal tap days in particular, Rachelle would struggle emotionally. On occasion she would take her feelings out on me, blaming me for what she was going through.

Spiritually, Rachelle took some time to review her decision to accept Christ as her Savior. With death a potential reality, she wanted to be sure that she would go to Heaven. She got that firmly settled in her heart early in the cancer battle. She had a great deal of faith that God would heal her.

Frequently, especially when struggling with the pain and nausea, she would sing songs. One of her favorites was a song she heard by Twila Paris, "Do I Trust You."

Sometimes my little heart can't understand
What's in Your will, what's in Your plan.
So many times I'm tempted to ask You why,
But I can never forget it for long.
Lord, what You do could not be wrong.
So I believe You, even when I must cry.
Do I trust You, Lord?
Does the river flow?
Do I trust You, Lord?
Does the north wind blow?

You can see my heart,
You can read my mind,
And You've got to know
I would rather die
Than to lose my faith
In the One I love.
Do I trust You, Lord?
Do I trust You?
I will trust You, Lord, when I don't know why.
I will trust You, Lord, till the day I die.
I will trust You, Lord, when I'm blind with pain!
You were God before, and You'll never change.
I will trust You. I will trust You. I will trust You, Lord.
I will trust You.

(Used with permission.)

✦✦✦

NAHUM 1:7

The LORD is good, a stronghold in the day of trouble; and he knoweth them that trust in him.

CHAPTER SIX

September 1990: My Journey

As the year passed into the fall season, the trials continued in other ways. In September 1990, the phone rang with a call from another doctor in Salt Lake City about me. He wanted to let me know that the mole I had removed from my forehead earlier that week turned out to be a malignant melanoma, stage two. These tend to be genetic in my family, and I have tried to be pro-active in watching moles on my body. When this one appeared to have some changes, I had it removed. When I received the phone call from the doctor that this one was malignant, I was reminded again to never ask, "What else can go wrong?" The potential for more surgeries, radiation, and even the possibility that Rachelle and I were going to have to go through treatments and wigs together for a while almost paralyzed me with fear again. Another surgery was scheduled for me to remove all the melanoma and nearby tissue on my forehead while we prayed and hoped that it had not metastasized. By God's grace, it was found early, and the second surgery was able to get it all. The only long-term effect was that I would be required to have ongoing checkups every three months in Salt Lake City. That was no problem, as we were already making two or three trips a month for Rachelle.

As mentioned earlier, I had scheduled with the Meniere's specialist in Denver, Colorado, to have brain surgery in November 1990. It was a frightening surgery to me, and I would have to go alone. Jamie was unable to leave Rachelle with her treatments in progress, so I asked my mother to fly up from Texas to be with me in Denver. The surgery went as expected, but I was put into a medically induced coma for a few days in order to let my brain heal. This was an unusual experience, as I could not open my eyes, move, or speak, but I could hear everything around me. To add to the experience, there was a nurse who apparently was assigned to me at night. I could not see her, but I recognized her voice. She knew I could hear her, although I was unable to respond verbally, and for at least two nights, she would come in repeatedly and quietly talk to me, telling me that she was a Satanist, a practicing witch, and that I should call on my "inner being" and open up to Satan! I do not know if she realized that I was a Baptist pastor's wife and was deliberately harassing me or if that was her practice to get vulnerable patients to be affected by demons, but as a born-again Christian, I was in full spiritual revolt to what she was saying. I simply was not physically able to respond verbally.

Finally, I had all I could take. I prayed for strength, and when she started again, I was able to yell at her, "Get away from me!"

I heard her shriek, "Oh!" and she left the room. She did not say anything more to me, but later, when I was able to see and speak again, I reported this to the floor nursing supervisor. When I checked out of the hospital a few days later, a hospital representative asked to meet with me. I did not know if they would give validity to my complaint or accuse me of being unstable due to the brain surgery. However, I was informed that other patients had made the same complaint about this nurse, and they wanted me to know that she had been terminated for her behavior. This was another reminder that, when we are most weak and vulnerable, Satan will try to attack. It's amazing to me that the enemy will try to challenge us so strongly, and yet it is more amazing to me how constantly good and great our God is! Physically, the surgery was successful and did improve the vertigo and dizziness I had been dealing with from the Meniere's.

✦✦✦

God Leads His Dear Children Along

HYMN BY G. A. YOUNG

Sometimes on the mount where the sun shines so bright,
God leads His dear children along;
Sometimes in the valley, in darkest of night,
God leads His dear children along.

Though sorrows befall us and Satan oppose,
God leads His dear children along;

Through grace we can conquer, defeat all our foes,
God leads His dear children along.

REFRAIN:

Some through the waters, some through the flood,
Some through the fire, but all through the blood;
Some through great sorrow, but God gives a song,
In the night season and all the day long.

CHAPTER SEVEN

December 1990: Christmas Letter

Although the trials appeared overwhelming, we were also enjoying many blessings. By our Christmas 1990 letter to friends and family, we were able to write that

> *Rachelle, herself, is very optimistic and up. She does everything she did before except PE, and few people even remember she's sick. She looks and feels great (except for a couple of days a month for chemo). Her friends have stood by her, and she hasn't had to suffer much of the "pushing away" of other kids that some kids with cancer have suffered. She's doing well in school and carries a full load, with three honors classes and honors choir, and*

> *had two Bs and the rest As on her report card. She loves high school. Other good things include the response of the community as well as our Christian family during all this. Rachelle was hearing from people all across the United States. Even now, eight months after her initial diagnosis, a week doesn't go by that we don't hear from someone letting us know they're still praying for her.*

Our church family was a wonderful support system for us during this time. When we were beyond ourselves, there was always someone to whom we could turn and lean. Our faith was the glue that held us together, knowing that God loves us in spite of our mess-ups, and that God had the ability to make Rachelle well and to keep our family intact. We knew that God was in control of the situation. In the Christmas letter, we reported,

> *Our church is doing better than ever. We're running almost double what we were last year and have seen several make decisions and families join the church. Even financially the church is doing much better and we should have our building and property paid off in just two months! We're excited about the church's spirit and growth.*

We also counted blessings from the year.

> *Despite the trials, this has also been one of the most positive years of our lives. The best news is how God has been so near to us in all this. We've felt His hand hold us every time we've needed it and seen Him*

work as only God can. We are learning not to take each other, or our children, for granted so much, but realize that they are gifts from God only loaned to us for a while. We had a wonderful summer vacation with many of Jamie's family coming up and enjoying Yellowstone and the Tetons with us. We've been in contact with many friends and family we hadn't seen in years. Please keep us in your prayers through the next year, as we will you.

Many Christians around the country had heard of our trial and were contacting us with promises of prayer. We created a prayer card with Rachelle's picture on it (taken a few days before her hair fell out) and included a verse from James 5:15, *"and the prayer of faith shall save the sick, and the Lord shall raise him up"* to send out as a thank-you note. We heard repeatedly that churches posted the prayer card and joined us in prayer for healing.

Thank you so much for praying for me. Please continue to keep me in your prayers for healing and strength.

"And the prayer of faith shall save the sick, and the Lord shall raise him up; ... The effectual fervent prayer of a righteous man availeth much." James 5:15-16.

Rachelle Jett
c/o Uinta Bible Baptist Church
P. O. Box 1316
Evanston, WY 82930

✦✦✦

JAMES 5:15–16

And the prayer of faith shall save the sick,
and the Lord shall raise him up; . . . The effectual
fervent prayer of a righteous man availeth much.

CHAPTER EIGHT

January 1991: The Ultimate Sacrifice

A new year was here, and winter was hitting hard. A full-blown blizzard came the day we were to go to Salt Lake City for another scheduled treatment. Interstate 80 was shut down, so we could not drive to the Primary Children's Hospital. Unsure what to do, we called the local Evanston hospital to see how to proceed. They called Primary Children's Hospital which instructed us go to our local doctor for blood work to see if Rachelle could have a treatment, as blood counts had to be at a specific level. Sure enough, the blood work came back as perfect for having the treatment and revealed that it needed to be done right away. The Primary Children's Hospital came up with a plan to have someone fly the chemo drugs to Evanston, and the local doctors could administer it. It sounded great! However, a couple of hours later, they called back. The storm was so severe that the flight carrying the necessary chemo drugs was diverted to another state, but they said there was a local pilot who had volunteered to fly the medications for Rachelle to Evanston in his private plane. This pilot had a heart for, and readiness to help, sick children and was willing to take the risk. We were amazed and blessed by this.

An hour or so passed, and we received another call informing us that the plane did not work out as hoped, and we needed to try to make the drive to Salt Lake City. We did not know how it was arranged, but the highway patrol opened up the interstate barricades so that we could drive on the highway, and we headed down through the mountains to the hospital. The drive was challenging in the blizzard, but my husband was now getting very good at navigating in the snow, and God's hand was on us. We arrived at the hospital without incident, and Rachelle received her treatment. As we were getting ready to leave the hospital, we asked some of the employees about the pilot. Hesitantly, with tears in their eyes, they told us he had been killed in a plane crash on the landing field near our home as he was trying to deliver the medicine for Rachelle. How heart-breaking! A man gave his life for a little girl he did not even know. What a picture and reminder of the sacrifice that Jesus gave. He gave His life for us in order that we can go to Heaven. We pray that pilot's family has experienced the ultimate gift Christ has given and been comforted in their loss.

Juggling the many types of medications, some of them classified as experimental, was a challenge for the doctors. On one treatment day at Primary Children's Hospital, Rachelle's head suddenly twisted up and around, her eyes rolled up into her head, and she became terribly frightened. The doctors became concerned and told us she was experiencing an oculogyric crisis as a side-effect of one of the drugs they had given her. One doctor told me that the condition could be permanently disabling and was unsure how this would progress. Rachelle was almost in panic mode, and I could only hold her hand and pray while the medical team worked on her, trying to resolve the problem.

Right in the middle of this crisis, friends arrived from out of town to visit with us, wanting to be an encouragement. Medical personnel would not allow them to come back in the room with us because of the severe nature of the crisis, so the friends asked if I would come out and talk to them. Rachelle did not want me to leave her, and I was torn as to what to do. They had driven far, and I didn't want to hurt their feelings. Should I leave Rachelle and go out to speak to them and, at least, thank them for coming? Rachelle frantically, repeatedly said, "Mom! Don't leave me!"

Finally, I told Rachelle, "I'll be right back," and I walked out to talk with the visitors for a few minutes to let them know what was going on. When I went back to Rachelle, the problem was still unresolved, and it was hours before it finally started improving. I could tell I had hurt Rachelle's feelings by leaving her for even a few minutes while she was so afraid. Even years later, when we reminisce of this time, one of Rachelle's memories is still "that time when Mom left me." Lesson learned? My priority should have been my daughter.

Day by Day

HYMN BY CAROLINA SANDELL BERG & OSCAR AHNFELT

Day by day and with each passing moment,
Strength I find to meet my trials here;
Trusting in my Father's wise bestowment,
I've no cause for worry or for fear.
He whose heart is kind beyond all measure
Gives unto each day what He deems best—
Lovingly, its part of pain and pleasure,
Mingling toil with peace and rest.

Ev'ry day the Lord Himself is near me
With a special mercy for each hour;
All my cares He fain would bear, and cheer me,
He whose name is Counselor and Pow'r.
The protection of His child and treasure
Is a charge that on Himself He laid;
"As thy days, thy strength shall be in measure,"
This the pledge to me He made.

Help me then in eve'ry tribulation
So to trust Thy promises, O Lord,
That I lose not faith's sweet consolation
Offered me within Thy holy Word.
Help me, Lord, when toil and trouble meeting,
E'er to take, as from a father's hand,
One by one, the days, the moments fleeting,
Till I reach the promised land.

CHAPTER NINE

Spring 1991: The Way Was Dark, and Then...

At the start of March 1991 everything seemed to settle into a kind of routine. Then a dark time began again, when Rachelle's heart rhythm became very unstable. The side effects of the treatments were affecting her more severely, and she was not able to bounce back physically between them as she had before. She would have bouts of depression, feeling as though she never got to do anything and that life was passing her by. Although the doctors recommended antidepressants, we chose not to take them, and God's Word became her help, as she was able to overcome those feelings. We combatted the depressive thoughts by focusing on counting blessings.

As the chemo treatments went on, the effects worsened. The vomiting became progressively more severe and lasted longer. The spinal taps became completely unbearable as scar tissue built up and caused the procedure to be more difficult, and it took longer to perform, while excruciatingly painful. The other side effects were also more pronounced. She suffered with a constant pounding headache, most likely from the spinal taps and chemo to her brain, about which the doctors could do nothing. Her heart arrhythmia became out of control, and no medicine seemed to help. A cardiac crisis came, and we rushed to the emergency room in Evanston, where she was admitted into the intensive care unit in our local hospital. The heart medicine was reacting against the chemo medicines, resulting in her blood pressure dropping to a point where it became a serious, life-threatening situation. At one point, one of the nurses frantically yelled, "We're losing her!" I was asked to assist them as they tried to revive her. I held her hand and prayed as the attending doctor tried to place a call to Primary Children's Hospital for emergency instructions and direction. Once again, God intervened, and she survived that particular crisis. Obviously, though, this was not working, and something had to change.

We were sent again to Salt Lake's Primary Children's Hospital. The cardiologists were now telling us that Rachelle needed urgent open-heart surgery to correct the heart arrhythmia before permanent damage was done, but the oncologist argued that she could not survive a surgery while on chemotherapy, and the cancer was still undefeated. One treatment day in March, Rachelle and I were at the Primary Children's Hospital again for a treatment. Honestly, we both felt we had completely reached the end of our ropes. The medical team members were arguing in front of us about what was needed next. Already anxious about the anticipation of another spinal tap scheduled for that day, Rachelle became hysterical. When the doctors left the room, she suddenly took off running, down the hospital halls, out the door, and across the parking lot. I was right on her heels, running after her and trying to get her to come back inside. Finally, she stopped and submitted to walk back into the hospital with me. Once I got her in the treatment room, my now fourteen-year-old daughter climbed into my lap and begged me to not make her go through anymore of this. "Please just let me die! Don't let them touch me!" she begged repeatedly.

My heart suddenly swelled in anger and rebellion toward the Lord. I felt God had left us, as negative thoughts filled my mind. *Where was His promise that we would not have to go through more than we could bear? We were living proof that was not true! I argued with and pouted at God. How could I teach Rachelle and our church members to walk in God's ways and claim His promises, if He did not fulfill them?* I had tried so hard to find blessings in everything and be thankful. However, I thought at this point that there was nothing for which I could be thankful. I truly considered picking her up, taking my daughter home, and giving up.

Then, as my heart filled with conviction and shame at what I knew were false accusations against my Holy God, I submitted to just watch—to wait and see what He would do—and to thank Him *in advance* for whatever He had for us. *I surrender all,* I prayed as I, in my heart, lifted Rachelle in my arms toward Him. *Whatever You decide, whatever You say, I will thank You.*

And then the blessings began. In a little while, the nurse came in and said, "Guess what? There is a brand new nausea drug that is being described as a miracle worker, and we're going to give it to Rachelle first before any of the other children in the hospital!" They started the medication, and it did help. In fact, after that, she never again suffered with severe nausea as she had in the earlier treatments.

♦♦♦

Whatever You decide,
whatever You say,
I will thank You.

♦♦♦

And then we headed down the hallway for the dreaded spinal tap. As we always did, I held her hand and repeated the Lord's prayer with her while they administered it. Miraculously, the spinal tap was one of the easiest she had ever had. In fact, she looked up at me when they were done and said, "Mom, I didn't even feel that one."

And then the cardiologist came in and told us they had found a new heart drug that they believed would not interfere with the chemo. This would get her heart under control, at least until the chemotherapy regimen was completed, and she could undergo the heart surgery. They dismissed us for the day, and we had an unusually good drive home with minimal nausea.

And then within a few short weeks' time, we were able to make one of the two memorable family trips that helped and encouraged us. The first, to Washington, D.C., was even more special to us because the entire community of Evanston raised the funds to enable our family to experience this amazing trip. A letter written to family and friends recounts our experiences.

> *Jason really put his heart into the spelling bee competition this year and won Wyoming state champion. That entitled him to compete in the National Spelling Bee in Washington, D.C., in May. None of us had ever been to Washington, so we determined that all of us would go except Joshua (who hates spelling bees and museums). We had a great trip to Washington and enjoyed tours to all the famous sights, memorials and museums for a week. Our entire family's favorite was the Smithsonian National Air and Space Museum. The spelling bee itself was an unbelievable experience too. Jason went out second round but was grateful that he didn't go out first round. Other fun things included riding the subway after we got over being afraid of it. We stayed at the Capitol Hilton just two blocks from the White House, but no, we didn't get to see the president or even Millie the dog.*

And then, on top of all this, we were notified that Rachelle had been granted a Make-A-Wish trip to Disney World in Florida for the whole family. This trip was made in the summer in conjunction with Rachelle's fifteenth birthday, July 16, 1991. What a wonderful experience! Rachelle was treated like royalty. We stayed in a beautiful house with a stocked refrigerator and all amenities, including a pool. We went to Disney World, Epcot Center, SeaWorld, and MGM Studios for six days. The experience meant everything to Rachelle and was an enormous encouragement. The trip was relaxing, enjoyable, full of good family memories, and (best of all) had nothing to do with doctors or hospitals.

After struggling through such a dark time, these blessings came all at once! God had the blessings waiting in the wings already, but I believe God waited until we saw that we were absolutely beyond ourselves and could not go on without His interventions. If He had not, we could have easily taken all the blessings for granted and would not have counted them as joy so that He would get the glory. Or what if we had given up? What if I had given in and said, "OK, it all stops here; no more treatments?" What if I had taken Rachelle home, stopped all treatment as she begged me to do, and let her die? If I had, I would not be able to tell you now that the doctors used the word *miracle* in relation to her multiple times. It takes the darkest night to make the light shine brightest. In the darkest night, our Heavenly Father shines in His work to free us from fear, give us strength, hold us up, and walk with us. May the true Shepherd's right hand of righteousness always get the glory for this!

♦♦♦

ISAIAH 40:28–31; 41:10

Hast thou not known? hast thou not heard,
that the everlasting God, the LORD, the Creator
of the ends of the earth, fainteth not, neither is weary?
there is no searching of his understanding.

He giveth power to the faint; and to them
that have no might he increaseth strength.

Even the youths shall faint and be weary,
and the young men shall utterly fall:

But they that wait upon the LORD shall
renew their strength; they shall mount up
with wings as eagles; they shall run, and
not be weary; and they shall walk, and not faint.

Fear thou not; for I am with thee;
be not dismayed; for I am thy God;
I will strengthen thee; yea, I will help thee;
yea, I will uphold thee with the
right hand of my righteousness.

CHAPTER TEN

Fall 1991: Tangible Fear

By September 1991, Rachelle was nearing the end of her scheduled chemo regimen, but she starting having some suspicious symptoms, such as sweating at night. When I told her local family doctor, he reluctantly responded, "It's back, and the prognosis is poor." He set an immediate appointment for scans in Salt Lake City again. The doctors had already told us that if the cancer came back during this treatment time, our only alternative would be a bone marrow transplant. I called the insurance company to find out the coverage and what I would need to do to get off work and started preparing for this.

Things did not go well during the scans. Rachelle would have to drink the liquid contrast dye in preparation for the scans, and yet the nausea would keep her vomiting it up. The only thing that was successful was when the nurses would put a tube through her nose into her stomach with a funnel at the end. I would stand and pour small amounts of the contrast into the funnel until it was all down, and stayed down. Finally, we were able to get the scans done. Rachelle was nauseated when the scans were finished, and we went back to her exam room in the oncology department to wait for the results.

Waiting on test results was one of the hardest things to endure while on this journey. Minutes feel like hours and hours like days, and the anxiety was almost palpable. On this occasion, rather than starting her chemo as scheduled, the nurses just kept us waiting and waiting in the exam room, which made things more confusing for us. We did not know what the delay was. Then we overheard them in the hall looking at an X-ray and saying, "See, it's back right here." We were heartsick and devastated. I started to shake all over, believing we had heard that the cancer was back. Rachelle started vomiting violently again from the stress, even though she had been given no chemo. We waited for three hours, with no one telling us what was happening and assuming the worst.

Finally, one of the doctors came in and said he wanted us to come back in the morning for more tests. I blurted out, "What was on the scans?"

He seemed surprised, then responded, "Oh, didn't anyone tell you? They were clear." I almost vomited on his shoes. No cancer? He said they were just trying to find out what was causing the symptoms, because they knew it was not the cancer, but no one realized that we had not been informed. Thankfully, Rachelle did not have anything physically wrong, but the stress and fear had already taken its toll on us emotionally. Another lesson learned? Our thoughts influence our emotions, which can affect us physically. Keeping your thoughts focused on truth is important.

The Lord has given the blessing of focusing on Him and His Word in Psalm 112:7–8, *"He shall not be afraid of evil tidings: his heart is fixed, trusting in the Lord. His heart is established, he shall not be afraid, until he see his desire upon his enemies."*

In October 1991, Rachelle finally had her last scheduled chemotherapy treatment. When a few weeks had passed, the time came for her follow-up scans. The realization that these would be the first scans since the chemo had been stopped paralyzed us with fear again. I worried, *Had the cancer come right back once the chemo treatment was discontinued?* Memories of the horror of the last scans would put me in a cold sweat. I finally prayed and told the Lord that, by His grace, I would not let it upset me so much again.

This time, the prep for the scans went smoother, and I left Rachelle to go out in the waiting room, as they would not let me be with her this time. I had done fine up to this point, with very little nervousness, but now sitting down, I felt that trembling feeling coming back. *Oh Lord, please don't let me get so upset again.*

I felt Him say to me, "Pull your Bible out of your purse and read it. That will help."

I argued, *But, Lord, the waiting room is packed with parents and children, and I'm too embarrassed to pull my Bible out and start reading. They'll think I'm being pious or something.*

"Get your Bible out," I heard Him tell me in my heart. *But, Lord...* Suddenly my purse tumbled off the chair where it was sitting next to me, causing my Bible to fall out of it and slide several feet across the floor. This resulted in everyone in the room jumping and turning to see what had happened. *Well, Lord, I guess if you want to go to that much trouble, I'll read my Bible! I don't know where You want me to read, so I'll just open it and read whatever is there.*

Obviously, I still was not having a proper spiritual attitude. However, I opened my Bible and my eyes fell on Psalm 103:2, where I began to read.

> *Bless the Lord, O my soul, and forget not all his benefits; who forgiveth all thine iniquities; who healeth all thy diseases; who redeemeth thy life from destruction; who crowneth thee with lovingkindness and tender mercies; who satisfieth thy youth with good things; so that thy youth is renewed like the eagle's.*

God spoke to my heart and said, "This is my promise to you!" After that, I did not care if everyone saw me reading my Bible because I was having a praise time to myself! I knew God told me that He had decided to heal her diseases, redeem her life, and renew her youth, and I did not have to bear the burden of not knowing whether the cancer would come back anymore.

Shortly after, the nurse came to get me, and of course, the scans came back all clear—no cancer! And the cancer never came back again. God had so graciously healed her and patiently, lovingly affirmed this to me through His Word.

+++

Dreams Fulfilled

A POEM BY RACHELLE, AGE 14

Did I fulfill my dream, or did I waste my time?
No, this dream is accomplished, I know, in my mind
I will have gone through and finished my treatments.
Will I be ready if I have to start again?
This time will it be cured, or will I have to go back in?
Can I handle the pain, and keep back the tears?
The first time was hard, in the hospital and on the bed.
Catching up on schoolwork after missing two days, I dread.
Will it all be worth it, in the end?
I think it will be.
I am alive, and well, you see,
With the help and support from my friends,
And other people with their mail.
My dream is fulfilled, and I am alive and well.

+++

ISAIAH 38:9–20

The writing of Hezekiah king of Judah,
when he had been sick, and was recovered of his sickness:

I said in the cutting off of my days, I shall go to the gates of the
grave: I am deprived of the residue of my years.

I said, I shall not see the LORD, even the LORD,
in the land of the living: I shall behold man no more
with the inhabitants of the world.

Mine age is departed, and is removed from me
as a shepherd's tent: I have cut off like a
weaver my life: he will cut me off with pining sickness:
from day even to night wilt thou make an end of me.

I reckoned till morning, that, as a lion,
so will he break all my bones: from day even to night
wilt thou make an end of me.

Like a crane or a swallow, so did I chatter:
I did mourn as a dove: mine eyes fail with looking upward:
O LORD, I am oppressed; undertake for me.

What shall I say? he hath both spoken unto me,
and himself hath done it: I shall go softly
all my years in the bitterness of my soul.

O LORD, by these things men live,
and in all these things is the life of my spirit:
so wilt thou recover me, and make me to live.

Behold, for peace I had great bitterness:
but thou hast in love to my soul delivered it
from the pit of corruption: for thou hast cast
all my sins behind thy back.

For the grave cannot praise thee,
death can not celebrate thee: they that go down
into the pit cannot hope for thy truth.

The living, the living, he shall praise thee,
as I do this day: the father to the children
shall make known thy truth.

The Lord *was ready to save me:*
therefore we will sing my songs to
the stringed instruments all the days of our life
in the house of the Lord.

CHAPTER ELEVEN

Christmas Letters Record the Journey

Christmas Letter, 1991

Rachelle has now been off chemotherapy since mid-October. She also has her driver's permit, babysits a lot, and is growing her own beautiful hair again.

A funny story: the shop classes at the high school had informal "elections" of high school girls, and Rachelle was elected as the "girl with the prettiest hair." They have no idea that it's a wig! (That's what they claim, at least.) Anyway, she's keeping her grades up and thinks it's great that she doesn't have to do everything as "catch-up" like she did last year. She enjoys working as a student aide in the high school office.

Jason's had a tremendous year too. In addition to winning the Wyoming State Spelling Bee, he is more sports minded than ever. He was All-Star first baseman in baseball, first string quarterback in football, and barely hanging in there in basketball. He was awarded Student of the Month in November by the Exchange Club which really tickled him and us both. Also, he has a job at the dog kennel, which is almost next door to our church, as the official "pooper-scooper." It's just a few hours once a week, or when they're busy, but he enjoys the spending money.

Joshua is in first grade now. Believe me, I was not sure I could say that just a few months ago. He really had trouble with talking and socializing too much (that's all he wanted to do) at the first of the year. We were afraid he might need to stay in T-1 before he tried first grade so that he could mature a little. He has really snapped out of it and is doing fine, now. He still enjoys socializing, however. Academically, he's where he should be, so we're glad we hung in there and didn't put him back. Naturally he's all excited about Christmas, and this year he gets to pass out the gifts because he can read!

Jamie is doing well. He really enjoyed hunting season this year and brought in two deer for our freezer with the new rifle he got for his birthday. He came in all excited one day because he had seen eight moose while he was hunting that morning. He actually got the opportunity to watch one of the bull moose go up to a cow moose and start kissing her (licking her nose, of course!) That may seem silly to you, but how many people can say they've seen two moose kissing in Wyoming?

Our church has grown in an amazing way. From our start with sixteen people, we now average one hundred every Sunday and almost always have visitors. Our church is now totally debt-free, as we burned our bank notes in February. We are almost done with a building program that doubled our church size and added a kitchen, a mission apartment, and several new classrooms. We were also blessed in the last few weeks with a 1991 van that is also debt-free. God's really good!

The best news I've saved for last as our best Christmas gift. This week Rachelle had her first follow-up tests since being off chemotherapy. They were totally clear, and the doctors gave us a very optimistic report! In fact, if her next scans in March are still clear, they will not need to do testing for several months.

> *This is a great gift to us; however, it is not as great as the gift given to us the first Christmas—our salvation. 2 Corinthians 9:15, "Thanks be unto God for his unspeakable gift."*

Jamie and I were excited to see how God allowed us to share what we were learning in multiple ways. One day, the doctors at Primary Children's Hospital asked us to meet with another family who had just learned of their child's cancer diagnosis and poor prognosis. We were honored to be asked to share our testimony and encouragement with another hurting family.

Rachelle was growing physically stronger once the treatments concluded, and her hair began to grow in. It came back curlier than before and with a gray streak in her bangs, but she felt wonderful having her own hair again.

Christmas Letter, 1993

> *The top news has to do with Rachelle. When she went to the doctors in September for her cancer check-up, they declared her cancer-free! What a miracle to hear those words! The doctors asked that she come once a year, do a minor blood test only, and follow-up for research only. They will not even be looking for the cancer anymore. They believe her chances of getting cancer again are the same as anyone else, because it would be a different cancer. The non-Hodgkin's lymphoma is completely gone!*

Her second big news came in the summer when she had a heart procedure done, called a catheter ablation, to repair the SVT that had become such a problem since she went on chemo. The wonder of this is that just recently, the doctors thought they would have to perform open-heart surgery to accomplish this. Technology has advanced so much, that the repair was able to be done with catheters and small incisions in her legs and shoulders. It took six hours, but she was out of the hospital within two days and riding horses within the week. The doctors say the SVT is completely cured as well, and they do not need to see her anymore.

Because of this trial, our family is closer, and we are less likely to take each other for granted. As teenagers, Rachelle and Jason seem more mature than many of their friends. We actually feel that what we've been through has been a blessing in many ways.

What an honor and a privilege to have been through this trial so that we could see God work in a personal way. Rachelle is living proof that God is all-powerful and still works miracles on our behalf. Sometimes, when I find myself bogged down and worried over something in my life, I can catch myself and say, "Do I really think God cannot handle this, when I've seen God cure cancer? I think we often sell ourselves short by trying to do things ourselves and not even giving God the opportunity to show His love and care for us.

✦✦✦

HABAKKUK 3:18–19

Yet I will rejoice in the Lord,
I will joy in the God of my salvation.

The Lord God is my strength,
and he will make my feet like hinds' feet,
and he will make me to walk upon mine high places.

CHAPTER TWELVE

August 1994: Jason's Journey

As we have already mentioned, Jason loved being involved in spelling competitions and sports. When fall football practice began in 1994, Jason did a self-examination to prepare for it and discovered a lump that was concerning. We took him to the doctor immediately to exam it, and we heard those dreaded words again "This is cancer." At sixteen years old, our son now had to face the same enemy that his sister had been fighting, although it was a different type of cancer. We were urgently sent back to Primary Children's Hospital in Salt Lake City for evaluation and treatment. The following day, Jason had a relatively minor surgery to remove the growth and then stayed overnight in the hospital to recuperate. The doctors initially told us they believed that the cancer was localized and that they had removed it all; however, later tests indicated that the cancer had metastasized. He was found to have advanced cancer that had spread to his abdomen. With this diagnosis, and due to his age, he was transferred from Primary Children's Hospital to University of Utah Hospital. The doctors there did major, full abdominal surgery to clean out the cancer in his abdomen and to remove some cancerous lymph nodes near his kidneys.

He was in the hospital for a very rough post-surgical nine days. The extensive abdominal surgery left him in extreme pain. For the first two days, he was almost delirious and out of his head with the suffering. I asked the nurses multiple times if there was not something they could do to help him. He was given pain medication intravenously into his spine to try to give him relief, but nothing seemed to help. Jamie came and brought a group of teenagers from Evanston to see Jason in the hospital, but Jason was so distraught and crying in pain that I would not let them in. Finally, after several hours, another medical staff member checked the IV in his back that was administering the pain medication and discovered that it had disengaged and was actually pouring all the pain medication into the mattress rather than into his body. No wonder! After correcting this, the pain became more manageable, but he continued to be miserable for several days.

Again, we were encouraged when the doctors told us they had removed all the cancer with the abdominal surgery. However, two weeks after the surgery, we received another phone call. We were told that the lab reports revealed that the cancer had continued to spread. The surgery had not removed it all and now it would show up either in his brain or in his lungs, which would put his life in jeopardy. The doctor recommended aggressive radiation and chemotherapy treatments start immediately; however, the treatments could cause irreparable damage to his kidneys and could compromise his ability to father children.

Previously, when our daughter had cancer, we had done everything the doctors told us to do—every treatment—but now we did not have peace that we should continue with the recommended protocol for Jason. When we prayed for direction, we all believed God told us to stop. So we told the doctors, "We stop here." We could not bring ourselves to have peace and accept these treatments, so we refused. The doctors then personally asked Jason, who had turned seventeen in September and was now legally old enough to make his own medical decisions. Jason also refused to go forward with the treatments. The doctors were upset with us and completely convinced that further treatment was needed. That was a very scary time. As a compromise, we agreed to go to the hospital to have tests and scans every two weeks in order to catch the cancer as early as possible wherever it showed up. Again, we were told that if they saw the cancer anywhere at all, treatment would start immediately, regardless of our hesitation.

For a while, Jason had a hard time dealing with the up-and-down reports we were getting. Entering his junior year in high school, he was scheduled to play varsity football and had been working out with weights all summer. He also was selected to be in an exclusive six-voice choir at the high school. Getting sick at the beginning of school knocked him out of both those things and was a huge disappointment to him. For a short period of time, Jason seemed to struggle with anger at everybody and everything. We sent him on a short trip to California to visit with Rachelle at the college she was now attending as a freshman (Pacific Coast Baptist Bible College) for a week. She was majoring in elementary education with a desire to teach and serve full-time in a church ministry. The students there were a very close-knit group with a sweet spirit and a desire to serve the Lord. Jason was greatly encouraged as the students invested and ministered to him. He returned home with a better attitude, ready to go forward.

Despite the health disappointments, other doors starting opening for him at school; he was inducted into the National Honor Society and made the All-State Choir. This, along with being in the Student Council gave him new areas in which to direct his energies. By Christmas, he was doing wonderfully, working part time at a fast food restaurant and paying for his "new" car, a 1967 Chevy Bel Air.

By another of God's miracles, Jason's cancer never raised its head again!

✦✦✦

PSALM 90:14–17

O satisfy us early with thy mercy;
that we may rejoice and be glad all our days.

Make us glad according to the days wherein
thou hast afflicted us, and the years
wherein we have seen evil.

Let thy work appear unto thy servants,
and thy glory unto their children.

And let the beauty of the Lord *our God be upon us:*
and establish thou the work of our hands upon us;
yea, the work of our hands establish thou it.

CHAPTER THIRTEEN

Guided by the Shepherd

As I paused to reflect on those four years, I realized that this journey had taught me some life-changing truths. The awesome God called Rachelle His innocent lamb. He would take her up in His arms as though a newborn lamb. He would lead me gently, as He would a nursing ewe burdened with the care of her young. He does love me. He does care. There were times when Satan would attack me with doubts. At times I would cry to the Lord, "Don't you love me? What's wrong with me that I'm unworthy of love? Why do you hate me so much?" But God does care, and He cares for you and me. *"Casting all your cares upon him, for He careth for you,"* 1 Peter 5:7 tells us. We might think, *That's not true. God does not care for me. I do not know why, but He doesn't.* But God said it. Can God lie? No, He cannot lie. Thus, the verse is true. God does care for us. When we were told our children had cancer, we were afraid. We did not even know how to pray sometimes. *Trust Him? But why? We have no idea how He could ever bring us through this.* And so we would cry out again, "O God! I'm scared and I do not even know what to ask." And God would hold us in His arms as a gentle shepherd would his lambs and answer, "Just trust Me." And so we did.

The Shepherd guided us as three family members were diagnosed with cancer in fewer than five years. Everyone we knew would ask us, "Why? Why do you have two children with cancer? Is it genetic? Is it environmental?" Even Joshua worried about this, and after Jason's diagnosis, went to his dad with obvious fear on his face and anxiously asked, "Dad, will I get cancer too?"

We have had genetic studies done on our family but have not learned anything definitive to date. In recent years, I have been diagnosed with breast cancer, which resulted in a lumpectomy with prescribed radiation treatment. This radiation treatment caused another rare cancer and necessitated further surgery. The genetic testing done in conjunction with this latest cancer revealed a gene that has been found to be associated with radiation-caused cancer. This certainly could be why God stopped us from accepting radiation treatment for Jason. Other than this, so far no doctors have been able to say that the cancers were anything other than "chance." This journey through multiple cancers and trials was in God's hands, and He has certainly taken care of us. We interpret that as God's will and readily accept that as the reason. We are, after all, the clay, and He

♦♦♦

This journey through multiple cancers and trials was in God's hands, and He has certainly taken care of us.

♦♦♦

is our potter (Isaiah 64:8). Does the clay ask the potter, "What are you doing" (Romans 9:21)? We believe, as Job says in 23:10, "When He hath tried me, I shall come forth as gold." Gold goes through fire not to be destroyed but to be purified and "re-formed" into something new. The purpose? That God would get the glory! That is our prayer in sharing our family's testimony—that God alone may get the glory. We have been faithfully, lovingly guided by God, our Shepherd.

✦✦✦

ISAIAH 40:11

He shall feed his flock like a shepherd;
he shall gather the lambs with his arm and carry
them in his bosom, and shall gently lead
those that are with young.

CHAPTER FOURTEEN

The Miracles Continue

Looking back now, it is even more evident that God's many miracles continue.

Rachelle is cured of cancer, married, and serves with her husband in full-time ministry. Because of the extensive surgeries and chemotherapy treatment, the doctors informed us that she would not be able to become pregnant and bear children. She and her husband were prepared for this when they married, so it was a complete surprise to learn that she was pregnant within only a few months of her marriage. She had an uneventful pregnancy and bore a healthy son. In hopes of more children, she had a complete workup by a fertility clinic that informed her that further pregnancy was not possible. She was told, "We don't know how you had him (her first son), but you won't have any more. You have no viable eggs in your body." Disappointed, but still desiring more children, they started making plans for adoption. Shortly after, however, she discovered she was pregnant again, and she bore another healthy son. Despite the doctors' prognosis that to have children would be impossible, she has borne two beautiful, healthy boys!

Jason is cured of cancer, as well. Despite the cancer battle, he finished high school and was named a National Merit Scholar. Believing God had placed a call upon his life, he also attended Bible college and is now, too, serving in full-time ministry. He and his wife enjoy a family of five healthy, beautiful children, despite the doctors' prognosis that he probably would not have children. Multiple miracles!

We have had the awesome blessing of hearing doctors say on multiple occasions, "This is a miracle. We don't understand. We can't explain, but..." God has worked multiple miracles in our lives. He gave His Innocent Lamb for us to have eternal life with Him in Heaven. He gave us our innocent lamb life lessons to show His power and healing while we live this life on earth.

All we can say is, "To God be the glory!"

✦✦✦

PSALM 107:20–22

He sent his word, and healed them,
and delivered them from their destructions.

Oh that men would praise the Lord *for his goodness,*
and for his wonderful works to the children of men!

CHAPTER FIFTEEN
Josh's Story

At nine years old, Joshua wrote a story about our family and submitted his perspective of this time for a school assignment called "My Family's True Story."

> *My family had a bad time. Well, when I was about four years old, we found out that my sister had blood cancer, and they said that she wouldn't live. She had CAT scans and surgeries and it was really tough. When she was done with a treatment, she came home and she threw up all night. This went on for a long time. My parents had a tough time too. I really hated it. My sister hated going through this. We thought she was going to die. She started getting better a couple of years later. They said her cancer was gone now. She is in college and is well,*

> *but when she had her cancer, she got a Make-A-Wish vacation to Disney World, Epcot Center, Sea World, and MGM Studios. It was really fun. Then we found out that my brother had cancer. He didn't get a Make-A-Wish because we already had one, but now almost all his cancer is gone and he is doing well. They are both doing very well now.*

Joshua also gave us an experience that taught and encouraged us to have perfect trust in the Lord. We had recently moved to Wyoming, and Joshua was barely four years old. His dad took him to fish on the bank of a large, deep river, the Hoback River. Josh has always loved to fish and has been successful at it since he was just a toddler. With his little Snoopy fishing pole in hand, Josh was standing beside my husband fishing. As my husband was casting, he heard a small splash and thought Joshua had either just thrown a rock into the river or had hooked a fish. When he turned, however, he couldn't see Josh anywhere. Surprised and puzzled, he looked down into the clear blue water, and there standing up on the bottom of the river, completely underwater, was Joshua. He was looking up at his dad with his big gray eyes. There was no fear on his face, and his arms were raised up in complete trust, as though saying, "Come get me, Daddy." He had no idea of the danger that he was in – only that he could see his father and knew his father would take care of him. So what did his father do? He was faced

♦♦♦

God wants us to respond to the overwhelming trials of life with no fear, arms raised in complete and perfect trust, eyes focused on Him, no matter what the circumstances.

♦♦♦

with a choice. Either wait and say, "Well, son, you got yourself into that situation, now get yourself out!" or he could get down on his hands and knees, reach into the water, and pull his son out of the potentially life-threatening situation. Of course that is what his father chose to do immediately. He pulled Joshua out of the water and, literally, set his feet on a solid rock. Joshua had water running from his nose and ears, yet he shook himself off like a wet puppy and without another word, simply picked up his fishing pole and started fishing again.

I know that's how God wants us to be with Him in our time of trial. David describes in Psalm 38:4 a feeling as though he is drowning, then in 38:15 he chooses to respond with, *"For in thee, O Lord, do I hope: thou wilt hear, O Lord my God."* God wants us to respond to the overwhelming trials of life with no fear, arms raised in complete and perfect trust, eyes focused on Him, no matter what the circumstances. Our loving Heavenly Father, the good Shepherd, will reach down, pull us out, save us from drowning, and set our feet on a solid rock.

✦✦✦

PSALM 91:1–16

He that dwelleth in the secret place of the most High
shall abide under the shadow of the Almighty.

I will say of the LORD, He is my refuge and my fortress:
my God; in him will I trust.

Surely he shall deliver thee from the snare of the fowler,
and from the noisome pestilence.

He shall cover thee with his feathers,
and under his wings shalt thou trust:
his truth shall be thy shield and buckler.

Thou shalt not be afraid for the terror by night;
nor for the arrow that flieth by day;

Nor for the pestilence that walketh in darkness;
nor for the destruction that wasteth at noonday.

A thousand shall fall at thy side, and ten thousand
at thy right hand; but it shall not come nigh thee.

Only with thine eyes shalt thou behold and see
the reward of the wicked.

Because thou hast made the LORD*,*
which is my refuge, even the most High, thy habitation;

There shall no evil befall thee, neither shall
any plague come nigh thy dwelling.

For he shall give his angels charge over thee,
to keep thee in all thy ways.

They shall bear thee up in their hands,
lest thou dash thy foot against a stone.

Thou shalt tread upon the lion and adder:
the young lion and the dragon shalt thou trample under feet.

Because he hath set his love upon me,
therefore will I deliver him: I will set him on high,
because he hath known my name.

He shall call upon me, and I will answer him:
I will be with him in trouble; I will deliver him, and honour him.

With long life will I satisfy him,
and shew him my salvation.

CHAPTER SIXTEEN

Sharing Lessons Learned

The Good Shepherd

BY JAMIE JETT

Living in Wyoming for almost ten years gave us numerous opportunities to see many flocks of sheep. We saw sheep being herded on ranches, gathered in fields, and being watched by a shepherd in his shepherd's wagon. Sheep would move down the highway, led by a shepherd in the back of a pickup as he lured them along with food pellets. In Wyoming, sheep on the highway always had the right of way. A vehicle would drive up to them slowly, and they would part like the Red Sea as it carefully maneuvered its way through the flock.

If you have ever researched sheep, you would have found that most of what has been written about them is not very flattering. They aren't the brightest of God's creatures. They are often referred to as dumb. Whether they are truly dumb or not, one thing is certain—God compares people to sheep in Isaiah 53:6, *"All we like sheep have gone astray; we have turned everyone to his own way..."*

- 1 Peter 2:25, *"For ye were as sheep going astray; but are now returned unto the Shepherd and Bishop of your souls."*

We have all "gone astray," which means we have all sinned and broken God's commandments.

There is a payment that must be made for our sins.

- Romans 3:23, *"For all have sinned, and come short of the glory of God;"*

Like the shepherd who watches over the sheep in the pasture, God desires to be a Shepherd to us and to take care of our needs. In fact, as the Good Shepherd, He cares for us so much that He sent His son Jesus to pay for our sin. Jesus laid down His life for the sheep.

- John 10:11, *"I am the good shepherd: the good shepherd giveth his life for the sheep."*

- Hebrews 13:20, *"Now the God of peace, that brought again from the dead our Lord Jesus, that great shepherd of the sheep, through the blood of the everlasting covenant."*

God laid on Jesus all our sin.

- John 3:16, *"For God so loved the world, that he gave his only begotten Son, that whosoever believeth in him should not perish, but have everlasting life."*

Because the good Shepherd loved us and died for our sin, we can have a new and wonderful relationship with Him.

- John 10:27–28, *"My sheep hear my voice, and I know them, and they follow me: And I give unto them eternal life; and they shall never perish, neither shall any man pluck them out of my hand."*

Jesus as the good Shepherd is alive today, and He is willing to save anyone who will choose to call upon Him for salvation.

- Romans 10:9–10, *"That if thou shalt confess with thy mouth the Lord Jesus, and shalt believe in thine heart that God hath raised him from the dead, thou shalt be saved. For with the heart man believeth unto righteousness; and with the mouth confession is made unto salvation. "*

The good Shepherd desires for you to be in His fold, His family, His care. However, He does not force Himself upon you. He calls and asks you to make the choice.

If you would like to receive Him as your Savior, you may pray this simple prayer: "Lord Jesus, I know that I am a sinner. I know that the payment for my sin is death. I also know that You died for my sin. I ask You, by faith, to come into my heart and to save me and give me eternal life."

If you trusted Christ as your Savior, please write the author and let her know of your decision. Jesus has now become the good Shepherd of your soul!

- John 10:7–11, *"Then said Jesus unto them again, Verily, verily, I say unto you, I am the door of the sheep. All that ever came before me are thieves and robbers: but the sheep did not hear them. I am the door: by me if any man enter in, he shall be saved, and shall go in and out, and find pasture. The thief cometh not, but for to steal, and to kill, and to destroy: I am come that they might have life, and that they might have it more abundantly. I am the good shepherd: the good shepherd giveth his life for the sheep."*

How to Deal with the Trials of Life

BY VICKIE JETT

When going through these trials, I found myself asking God, "How do you want us to deal with the trials of life?" First, God led me to 2 Corinthians 7:4, *"I am filled with comfort, I am exceeding joyful in all our tribulation."* This "exceeding joyful" is also described as being "cheerful toward." At first the idea that I could respond to the trials as exceeding joyful seemed impossible. When we're going through trials, we may say, "You just don't understand. I can't possibly be happy about this situation." You may be right. You've probably heard that happiness is based on happenings and the saying is true—happiness comes from *outward circumstances.* Joy, on the other hand, comes from within; it is an *inward delight.* It has been defined as a steadfast confidence in God regardless of one's circumstances. Anyone can feel happy, but joy comes with experience. God is true, and His Word is true. How could this trial be turned to joy?

Choose to have joy by doing what God says. Obey God's Word, and take action.

1. **Take action to count it all joy (count your blessings). How can we do that?**

   James 1:2–4, "*Count it all joy when ye fall into divers temptations. Knowing this, that the trying of your faith worketh patience.*"

2. **Take action to give thanks for everything.**

   2 Thessalonians 5:18, "*In everything give thanks; for this is the will of God in Christ Jesus concerning you.*"

   Ephesians 5:20, "*Giving thanks always for all things unto God and the Father in the name of our Lord Jesus Christ.*"

God does not say to be thankful (a heart feeling); He says to give thanks, an action.

> Note: *All* is the overall picture. Every *thing* is the small details. For example: I had to learn to look for things to thank God for everything. This is not easy, but we must make it a practice to find something for which to thank God in every situation. For example, "overall" = cancer; "little" = cards, calls, pillows, slippers, and so on.

How often? Always. How much? All. Not just when I feel like it.

Why is this important? Because Psalm 22:3 tells us that God inhabits His praise.

When we praise Him, He is there.

3. Take action to look for things for which to praise the Lord.

Make a blessing notebook. Take action to look, then write down three different things, three times a day, every day. And try to not repeat. Writing these three things will change how you view the trial. It will provide a record upon which you can look back after the trial is passed and see how God blessed and provided for you.

4. Take action to sing.

Joy and singing go hand in hand. Sing the hymns. Ephesians 5:19 says, "*Speaking to yourselves in psalms and hymns and spiritual songs, singing and making melody in your heart to the Lord.*" Singing will change your heart in the trial. Have a song that is readily available when you need it, that will help you focus on the words and melody rather than on the present trial. Singing brings joy, and joy is what God desires for us. I am reminded of the chaffinch. A chaffinch is a bird found in England. It sings like a canary. However, it can forget its song. If it does, it dies. To save the bird's life, someone must carry it back into the woods to hear other canaries sing in order for it to get its song back and live. We, too, need to live with a song in our heart.

5. When you can't see anything for which to thank God, choose to thank God in advance for what He will do (by faith and obedience.)

Are you going through a trial now? If you are not right now, you will be.

Many of you are going through trials. It may not be cancer, but it may be just as hard for you—the loss of a loved one, the change of residence when we do not want to move, wayward children, unkind false rumors, ill health. In 2 Corinthians 12:9–10, we find that Paul had been complaining about his trials, and the Lord responded to Paul. *"And He said unto me, My grace is sufficient for thee: for my strength is made perfect in weakness."*

Paul replies back to the Lord. *"Most gladly therefore will I rather glory in my infirmities, that the power of Christ may rest upon me. Therefore, I take pleasure in infirmities* (illness), *in reproaches* (insults), *in necessities* (finance problems), *in persecution* (treated unjustly), *in distresses* (narrow, closed in, trapped) *for Christ's sake; for when I am weak, then am I strong."* Take action to give glory and take pleasure in every trial like Paul did.

Be patient. Remember the first part of James 1:2–4, *"Count it all joy when ye fall into divers temptations."* But it continues on—*"Knowing this, that the trying of your faith worketh patience."* Patience submits to God's timeline, not yours.

No matter what the trial, if you are a Christian, you can choose to count it all joy. Choose to respond like Paul by being exceeding joyful. Take action to count your blessings and to change your attitude. Be thankful for His love, presence, joy, strength, mercy, and grace. Learn to thank Him for what you cannot see. Allow God to walk you through the trial. Sing songs to Him, and give God the glory.

Reflections
BY VICKIE JETT

How Can We Count Blessings in Times of Trials?

In the beautiful mountains of Wyoming, people often still pan for gold (including some of our church members). To accomplish this, they take a shallow dish, scoop up some mud from the shallow edge of a stream, and then swish the water and mud around. As they do this, they pour out the dirt and look for flecks of gold, and gold is often found, along with other precious stones. The water is ice cold, and of course, the person panning gets wet and muddy, as well as tired from the bending over and using the same arm movement. But to find a nugget of gold! That makes the effort worthwhile. It's the same with looking for the gold of God when we're in a trial. It may take a little effort, and we might even be a little uncomfortable in the process, but the gold is worth the hunt. When going through a trial, practice looking for things "in the mud" to be thankful for. If all you can see is the mud, then learn to thank God for the mud itself. After all, the mud is nourishment to plants and is a medium for growth. No matter how bitter the trial, search out the treasure and thank the Lord for it.

Look for Beauty in the Scars

While living in Wyoming, I took a wildflower class from the local college. We went on field trips to mountains and alpine meadows and saw many beautiful flowers. One day, the instructor took us to walk along the interstate, and we came upon a pile of debris left from when the interstate was built: rocks and concrete and road garbage. Called "slag," it was ugly and distracted from the beauty of the natural landscape. However, the instructor told us to walk around and through it to look for flowers. Sure enough, we found an exquisitely beautiful little flower that flourishes among the slag environment and nowhere else. This flower really affected me—without the ugly scarring conditions, that flower would not survive, bloom, and beautify its surroundings. God brought unique beauty to the scar, and I have never viewed those ugly piles of slag the same since. There is beauty found in every scar.

Practical Suggestions: How to Help Those Who Are Hurting

Do:

- Pray, pray, pray. Those affected may not be able to pray at times. The prayer of faith speaks of *others* praying.
- Just be there. Don't avoid that person. Be the friend you've always been.
- Give a loving touch. A simple squeeze of the hand or a hug says you still care.
- Encourage each one to talk and then listen. Don't tell about everyone else you know with cancer. When someone is engulfed in a serious illness or trial, that person's mind doesn't have room to squeeze in much else. They need to express.

Don't

- Don't be afraid to visit. Sometimes the person is lonely, but do keep visits short.

- Don't get angry if the person is unable to talk to you when you visit. Be understanding if the person says no. Sometimes they are dealing with pain or even a sterile situation.

- Don't be impatient or critical of how that person is handling the situation.

Hospital Do's:

- If visiting with someone staying in the hospital, do not control the TV. Let that person decide what they are comfortable with. You're there to meet that person's needs, not yours.

- Be sensitive to doctor visits. When the doctor comes, step out. If the person wants you to stay, be quiet. Take notes, if requested. To get the doctor while one can is crucial.

- Be sensitive to modesty issues. Step out of the room so that the person can go to the bathroom. When arriving for a hospital visit, have the husband or wife step into the room first to see if the patient is modest and able to have visitors.

- In the hospital, good things to bring include the following:

  — Books, magazines, and light reading help pass the time.

  — Scented lotions and gum can make a person feel fresher.

  — Air freshener for the hospital room makes the room feel less sterile.

  — "Real" food is a nice break during long stays in the

hospital. Bringing in a pizza or tacos is nice unless that person is on a restricted diet. You may also want to arrange for family members to eat in the hospital cafeteria, as they may not have the funds or are unable to leave the hospital. A basket of treats (crackers, cheese, cookies, fruit, granola bars, etc.) is nice, too.

— Small, comfortable pillows or slippers are welcome.

— Thank-you notes, blank cards, and stamps let people keep others up to date.

— A tablet with a pen tied to it to lets family members write down doctors notes and visitors' names.

- Look for ways to help and make suggestions such as the following:

— Offer to watch children.

— Remember this can be at odd hours—emergencies seem to happen at the most inconvenient times. Also, remember that the other children in the family can be suffering now, too by feeling afraid and insecure. Be sure to be positive and encouraging around them.

— Chauffeur them to the doctor or take the kids to their activities.

— Clean the house or do the laundry. (But no telling what you saw!)

— Meals or treats are always nice. Everyone has to eat, but always bring in a disposable dish. Call ahead and let them know that you're bringing their favorite dish and what time you're coming.

— Call for a shopping list, and make a "special delivery" to the home. (toilet paper, milk, eggs, etc.)

— Take care of animals, pets or livestock.

- Think of others in the family. For example, if a child is ill, do something special for the siblings.
- Offer humor. Laughter is healing, too. Give funny cards, videos and books when you can. Proverbs 17:22, *"A merry heart doeth good like a medicine."*
- Money is nearly always a blessing. Even with good insurance, there are always bills to pay, travel expenses, meal expenses, special clothing (such as clothes for the hospital for the ill or the caregiver).
- Be patient. Don't set your own timeline for healing. Healing can take time and each person has a different timetable. Prayer is needed for the entire time.
- Use words to help, not hurt. Proverbs 12:18, *"There is that speaketh like the piercings of a sword: but the tongue of the wise is health."*

Let your words be sweet not tart. Proverbs 16:24, *"Pleasant words are as an honeycomb, sweet to the soul, and health to the bones."*

Don't Say (Tart)

- "Examine your heart and life. It may be God is judging you for some sin."
- "I know just how you feel." (You don't.)
- "Things could be worse."
- "Romans 8:28 is still true; you will just have to accept the will of God."
- "You've just got to be strong."
- "Time will heal."
- "It will be better soon."
- "Call me if you need anything." (They won't.)
- "I know someone else with cancer and they..."
- "I personally think chemotherapy is of the devil, and I believe you should..."

  (Unless they ask, don't push your remedies and express your cures. Treatment decisions are personal; they are between them and the Lord. With our daughter, we felt God's leading to do everything the doctors recommended, and some people criticized us for putting her through so much. We frequently had people recommend that we take her to Mexico for laetrile treatments and other remedies.

With our son, we felt led to refuse the radiation and treatment that the doctors recommended. God blessed every scenario. You might personally think chemotherapy is "wicked" and that only natural herbs should be used. Unless asked for advice, sharing your opinion may add to an already heavy load.)

- Death: "Your loved one is better off out of this wicked world." "At least he didn't suffer."
- If a baby or child dies: "You can always have another one." "At least you never got to know him." "It's probably for the best."

Do Say (Sweet)

- "I've been praying for you." (if true)
- "Is there something specific I should be praying for?"
- "I feel for you during this difficult time."
- "This must be very hard for you."
- "I want to help you; I'm available anytime you need me." (if true, of course)
- "I care."
- "Can I share a verse that blessed me today?"
- "Can you use a laugh?" (Proverbs 17:22)
- "Tell me about your day." (Then listen.)

- "Can you use a hug?"
- Death: "I'm sorry. I know how special she was to you." "I'll miss her also." "I remember when she…"
- Loss of a child: "I know how much being a mother means to you."

Move from Selfishness to Self-Sacrifice

BY VICKIE JETT

When faced with the trials of life, we can be tempted to respond with self-pity, self-focus, and selfishness. The answer to these "self" problems is self-sacrifice. To sacrifice is defined as, "To give something valuable or important for somebody, or to God, without any expectation of a reward."

Romans 12:1–2 tells us that we are to present ourselves as living sacrifices.

Philippians 2:17, *"Yea, and if I be offered upon the sacrifice and service of your faith, I joy, and rejoice with you all."*

The call to sacrifice can be a bit scary. If I sacrifice my*self,* what will happen to me? If you are like me, we want to think we are in control and we want to take care of our own needs. But God says we need to sacrifice "self" in order to have God's leading and to be able to minister to others. Especially in times of trials, we can be tempted to selfishness, self-focus, and self-pity.

Do we have needs? Sure we do. Let's think about this. The Lord, our Creator knows, and cares, about our needs. In fact,

Philippians 2:1–21 gives things that I feel sure you would need and want to have. Let's look at this passage to see if we can find five things we need.

Verse 1, *"If there be therefore any consolation in Christ, if any comfort of love, if any fellowship of the Spirit, if any bowels and mercies."* Are these things we need?

1. Consolation—exhortation, encouragement in Christ.

2. Comfort—to soothe, ease, and cheer.

3. Love/agape—godly, unconditional love.

4. Fellowship/communion—Talk and listen to our family and friends.

5. Bowels and mercies—tender emotion and compassion.

What a wonderful promise to have these needs met. However, God starts that verse with "if," four times, as though these things are conditional on something before we can receive them. Let's read verse 2 to find out how.

"Fulfil ye my joy, that ye be likeminded, having the same love, being of one accord, of one mind." We're commanded to be "likeminded, same love, one accord, one mind." The key word here is *one*. This must be important to God. Aren't we doing that? Let's look at verse 21, *"For all seek their own, not the things which are Jesus Christ's."*

Ouch! God said that *all* seek their own. If that is true, then it is impossible to be "likeminded, one love, accord, mind," isn't it? It sounds as if God is accusing us of being selfish. And if we're selfish, we do not qualify to receive the wonderful promises of verse 1.

You may justify this by saying, "I have needs. I have to look out for myself. If I don't, no one else will." That's what the world says, too. That is the opposite of what God says. God knows we have needs—He even lists them here. What He is saying is that if we are selfless and stop trying to get things for ourselves, our way, then God will meet these needs. He wants us to have these needs met and Philippians 2:1–21 is a guide. Here, He begins to tell us what to do to, so let's follow His instructions. We need to sacrifice our *self*. To do that, we need to put off some things and put on some things.

Verses 3–5 give five things to put off. We need to be cleaned, purged. Sometimes, the cleaning and purging we go through in life are not all pleasant, but they must be done, and we can rest in the fact that we know Christ means it for good.

Verses 3 and 4, "*Let nothing be done through* (1) *strife or* (2) *vainglory; but in lowliness of mind let each esteem other better than themselves. Look not every man on his* (3) *own things, but every man also on the things of others.*"

Let's start with purging the inside.

1. Strife—conflict with others/contention. This is strife on the inside. Thoughts focused on self.

2. Vainglory—promoting self over others; but in humility (lowliness of mind), esteem (consider) others better than self.

3. Look not on your own things (focus on self rather than on others)—It is not what I believe is needed, what I want, what I think, or what I feel. Rather, focus on others' needs: "What do they need, want, think?"

These three things are internal heart conditions. The next two are external—what happens when the heart condition shows up on the outside.

Verse 14, "*Do all things without* (4) *murmurings and* (5) *disputings:*"

4. Murmuring—complaining to self and others/grumbling/gossiping. Some thoughts to consider: Have you been wallowing in self-pity? Thinking about and listing all the bad things that have happened to you? How hard has your life been?

5. Disputing—debating/discussing/arguing with others.

Can you see the progression? (1) strife: selfish thoughts; (2) vain-glory: promoting self; (3) look not on your own things: focus on oneself, self-pity; (4) murmuring: complaining; and (5) disputing: fighting with others.

What is the import of responding to trials with selflessness? Verse 15 says, "*that we may be blameless and harmless.*" What is the harm if we're selfish anyway? Our selfishness, self-pity and self-focus affects not only ourselves but also others. This includes family, friends, and co-workers.

How can we change selfishness to selflessness? Look at verses 5–9. The Bible gives us Christ as our example.

Verse 5, *"Let this mind be in you, which was also in Christ Jesus: Who, being in the form of God, thought it not robbery to be equal with God: But made himself of no reputation, and took upon him the form of a servant, and was made in the likeness of men."*

The answer is to put on the mind of Christ, to put off the negative thoughts we've been thinking and to put on thinking the way God thinks. The Bible even tells us five things to put on.

1. Humble self.

Remember, we are putting on Christ's thoughts. Verse 3 also told us to have "lowliness of mind"—humility. The first thing said of Christ (verse 7) was that he gave himself no reputation. (*or glory to self*—the opposite of vain glory) and that He "humbled himself" (verse 8).

The opposite of humility is pride. Our pride is the base for our unwillingness to sacrifice our self. Confessing our sin of pride to God and to others can be very humbling and very helpful. A time of accurate self-appraisal is humbling and can reveal how focused we are on our self. One needs to see one's self as a sinner, a follower of Christ and under biblical authority.

Stop focusing on self; instead, focus on God and...

2. Think and focus on others.

Verse 3, *"Esteem* (consider) *others better than self."* (Put them first.)

Verse 4, *"Look on things of others."* Determine to pay attention and focus on others to know how to meet their needs.

3. **Serve others.**

Verse 7, He became a servant (voluntarily submitted). Sacrifice self to serve others, just as Christ did. Look to Jesus as our example to follow.

4. **Hold forth the Word of life.**

From verse 16. This means to hold forth the Bible to others. First, we must read the Bible to learn to think more like Christ, rather than be selfish, self-focused people. The Word of God and the preaching of it can guide us as we step out beyond ourselves to minister to others, whether with time, effort, or resources.

5. **Rejoice and praise.**

Verse 17 (and 3:1), *"Finally, my brethren, rejoice in the Lord."* Rejoice—look for and think on praise. Praise God every day! Sing songs to the Lord. When you realize how much God has done for you and continues to do for you, it's easier to trust Him as you sacrifice yourself.

What has God done for you? He gave His Son (verses 8–12). Salvation is the prerequisite to all this.

Verses 8–12, *"And being found in fashion as a man, he humbled himself, and became obedient unto death, even the death of the cross. Wherefore God also hath highly exalted him, and given him a name which is above every name: That at the name of Jesus every knee should bow, of things in heaven, and things in earth, and things under the earth; And that every tongue should confess that Jesus Christ is Lord, to the glory of God the Father."*

Jesus sacrificed everything for you. Let me ask here: Reader, do you know Christ as Savior? If not, then please allow this testimony to encourage you to look to Jesus for His help and healing.

Christian, when we think about what He did for us, how can we be selfish, self-focused? Because He died for us, can we not sacrifice ourselves for Him daily (1 Peter 2:24; 1 Corinthians 15:31)? Choosing salvation is once, but dying to self is daily.

When we sacrifice our self, we can minister to others. Verse 15 tells us that when we are one with others (not self-focused) we can *"shine as lights in the world."* Not only will we have joy but also family, friends, and others will joy and rejoice with us. That's what Paul said in verse 17, *"Yea, and if I be offered upon the sacrifice and service of your faith, I joy, and rejoice with you all."* Through self-sacrifice, others' needs are met, and we have our needs met!

1. Consolation

2. Comfort

3. Love

4. Fellowship

5. Bowels/mercies

Will you by faith, submit yourself to go through trials and live a life of sacrifice, not selfish, self-pitying, and self-focused?

✦✦✦

Savior Like a Shepherd Lead Us

HYMN BY DOROTHY THRUPP & WILLIAM BRADBURY

Savior, like a shepherd lead us,
Much we need Thy tender care;
In Thy pleasant pastures feed us,
For our use Thy folds prepare:
Blessed Jesus, blessed Jesus,
Thou hast bought us, Thine we are;
Blessed Jesus, blessed Jesus,
Thou hast bought us, Thine we are.

We are Thine, do Thou befriend us,
Be the guardian of our way;
Keep Thy flock, from sin defend us,
Seek us when we go astray:
Blessed Jesus, blessed Jesus,
Hear, O hear us when we pray;
Blessed Jesus, blessed Jesus,
Hear, O hear us when we pray.

Thou hast promised to receive us,
Poor and sinful though we be;
Thou hast mercy to relieve us,
Grace to cleanse, and pow'r to free:
Blessed Jesus, blessed Jesus,
Early let us turn to Thee;
Blessed Jesus, blessed Jesus,
Early let us turn to Thee.

Early let us seek Thy favor,
Early let us do Thy will;
Blessed Lord and only Savior,
With Thy love our bosoms fill:
Blessed Jesus, blessed Jesus,
Thou hast loved us, love us still;
Blessed Jesus, blessed Jesus,
Thou hast loved us, love us still.

Made in the USA
Las Vegas, NV
29 March 2022

46528353R00079